What people are saying about

How the Establishment Lost Control

An important and perceptive history of post-war Britain and the effects of neoliberalism. A critique with a robust philosophical basis, it explains where the inequalities that led us to this point originated, how they are being perpetuated, and how they can be deconstructed. Essential reading for anybody wishing to understand the state we're in.
Brian Eno

This is a book to cheer you up. The game's afoot. The old certainties are fading. The market doesn't work. People's lives are dominated by insecurity and pressures of all kinds. Can we bring together all who resist to make a real change? Chris Nineham argues for that possibility. It is a test not only of our determination, but also of our understanding. ...."
Ken Loach

A highly readable, fast moving account of how the British establishment has lost the plot. Chris Nineham reveals, often using their own words, that they know they have, but they would rather you didn't hear it from him or listen to the solutions he and so many others now suggest.
Danny Dorling, author of *Inequality and the 1%*

A must read for anyone concerned with the state of our times, its historical antecedents and the possibilities of a different world.
Alpa Shah, author of *In the Shadows of the State*

A clear guide as to how the elite

it can't get us out of it again, and it will stimulate debate as to how the left should respond.

Andrew Murray, author of *The Imperial Controversy* and *Off the Rails*

A provocative intervention into contemporary politics. Chris Nineham shows how 40 years of neoliberal capitalism resulted in accumulation by dispossession and the accumulation of discontent. The book makes an argument for socialism as the only adequate political response to the ongoing crises.

Christian Fuchs, author of *Critical Theory of Communication* and *Reading Marx in the Information Age*

How the Establishment Lost Control

The Left and the Return of Mass Politics

How the Establishment Lost Control

The Left and the Return of Mass Politics

Chris Nineham

Winchester, UK
Washington, USA

First published by Zero Books, 2017
Zero Books is an imprint of John Hunt Publishing Ltd., Laurel House, Station Approach,
Alresford, Hants, SO24 9JH, UK
office1@jhpbooks.net
www.johnhuntpublishing.com
www.zero-books.net

For distributor details and how to order please visit the 'Ordering' section on our website.

Text copyright: Chris Nineham 2017

ISBN: 978 1 78535 631 5
978 1 78535 632 2 (e-book)
Library of Congress Control Number: 2017932040

A CIP catalogue record for this book is available from the British Library.

Design: Stuart Davies

Printed and bound by CPI Group (UK) Ltd, Croydon, CR0 4YY, UK

We operate a distinctive and ethical publishing philosophy in
all areas of our business, from our global network of authors to
production and worldwide distribution.

Contents

Acknowledgements

This short book is more of a collective effort than most. As far as I am aware, the case for the the emergence of the kind of deep economic, social and political crisis of British capitalism outlined here was first sketched out in detail by Adrian Cousins in his prescient article 'The Crisis of the British Regime', and in a rather different way by Danny Dorling in his path-breaking book *Injustice*. Thanks to both these authors for providing me with so much ammunition for the pages that follow. Many others have of course elaborated different aspects of the unfolding crisis since. I am in debt to many of them and in particular to all those on the editorial board of Counterfire.org whose running commentary on the regime's unravelling has been invaluable. I am lucky enough to work with a group of activists and analysts in the Stop the War Coalition whose insights into the increasingly volatile world we live in are always enlightening. Responsibility for all that follows is mine, I would like to give special thanks to Dave Randall, Des Freedman, Chris Bambery, Feyzi Ismail, Lindsey German and John Rees for their comments on early drafts. I dedicate the book to Feyzi Ismail, one of the most critical readers of drafts, who I love dearly.

Introduction

Surprise, Surprise

The society of those in power really believes in its eternal duration.
Heinrich Heine[1]

The British establishment is reeling. For years the elites have been behaving as if serious opposition to their plans had disappeared. Many commentators, including some on the left, internalised ruling class over confidence and worried that no alternative to the free market economic model could ever take hold of the popular imagination again. Elite consensus was equated with commanding authority and any challenge to that authority was judged hopeless. Now there is disarray. 'The people' no longer seem enthralled by a future of endless globalisation. And they are not doing what they are told.

Instead they have delivered a series of shocks to the system. A narrow miss for Scottish independence in 2014, Jeremy Corbyn's leadership bid, the Brexit vote and Labour's spectacular June 2017 general election surge have generated the biggest crisis in British society since 1945. Consternation has grown as shocked commentators across the spectrum sought explanation for these upsets in the rise of xenophobia, populism or general unreason. Many took the Brexit vote in particular to express simply an outbreak of reactionary small mindedness amongst 'the white working class' or a turn towards narrow protectionism. Even some of the more radical critics of the neoliberal order have tended to assume that a 'sudden fracturing' of politics would automatically lead to a slide into 'political and cultural particularism' and a society split by 'cultural and national difference'.[2]

The 2017 general election forced some to begin to recognise

1

the roots of insubordination in a more rational rejection of an economic and political order. But there is still widespread wonderment. These multiple rebellions should not surprise. This short book argues they are expressions of a multi-level crisis in British society that has been germinating for decades. Popular anger has reached breaking point recently, but it never went away, even in the darkest times. For all the triumphalist rhetoric of Thatcher and her supporters, the majority of the population never signed up for the free market experiment and were never convinced by neoliberalism in action. For most, the Thatcher years were experienced as bleak and bitter, and in spite of the bribes and bullying, most continued to aspire to a more equal and caring society. Some on the left took the view that Thatcher had won hearts and minds, but at different times millions campaigned against her policies, and polls show that opposition grew even as the neoliberal regime bedded down. Thatcher's staying power was more the product of defeat, demoralisation and disorientation than it was of any popular buy-in.

The subsequent history of neoliberalism is one of the steady accumulation of anger and alienation, barely registered in polite society. Rocketing inequality and deepening poverty have been recorded at the margins of public debate but rarely regarded as particularly significant because, for those in a position to comment publicly, they weren't. Anger at venal politicians, anxiety about a disintegrating welfare state and outrage at a series of disastrous foreign wars has been briefly noted, but the official narrative always moves quickly on to less troublesome matters. More recent events have intensified indignation. The central idea of the whole paradigm – that the market knows best – took an absolute pummelling in the banking crisis of 2008. In that moment of panic, the authorities were unable to conceal that fact that their beloved market mechanisms took the whole economic system to the very edge of collapse. State neutrality was also exposed as a sham as, heaping insult upon injury, the champions of the small state responded to meltdown with massive state bailouts for the perpetrators of the crisis and used the shock to justify the launch of 'austerity'. Not only had ruling class messaging gone haywire, not only had its whole economic project been exposed as a shocking failure, but it wasn't even contemplating a change of course. As the dust settled and life continued, a relieved media was content to recycle official disclaimers and carry on as if nothing much had happened.

Is it really any wonder the country is in a state of mutiny? Despite the confused public debate, actual studies of public opinion showed that all the recent rebellions, for all their complexities and contradictions, were linked to growing outrage at inequality and social injustice. At first there was an instinctive element to this that outstripped conscious political positioning, in which many supporters of all political parties swung around to supporting renationalisation, increased taxes for the rich and an end to foreign wars – all normally regarded as left wing ideas, without necessarily changing political allegiance. But the general election of 2017 revealed something much more alarming for the elites. Millions of people have now developed the beginnings of a joined up critique of the prevailing economics and the way it has impacted on society, and they have started to identify with socialism and the left.

Of course politics is polarising, and relentless bombardment of the public by the media and the political elite with anti-immigrant and anti-Muslim propaganda has encouraged a nasty, zenophobic current in British society. As the elites get more desperate expect even more hysterical attacks on minorities. But the idea that society is careering to the right was never plausible. The Tories under a right wing leader were the biggest party after the June 2017 election, but not only was their majority much reduced, one of the many interesting and heartening things about the result was the fact that immigration wasn't one of the electorate's main concerns. What is more, the red baiting of Jeremy Corbyn, his team and allies didn't stop the biggest swing to Labour since 1945. Nearly 13 million people voted for the most left wing Labour manifesto in a generation. Despite defeat, the initiative was with the left.

State of denial

Clearly the establishment is losing its persuasive powers. During the Scottish Independence campaign, Corbyn's rise, Brexit and the general election we were blessed with highly orchestrated and extravagantly funded campaigns of propaganda and persuasion, mobilising elite voices from across what passes for a political spectrum, gaining the overwhelming support of the mainstream media in three of these cases, and the majority, especially the broadcasters, in the case of Brexit. To the elites' shock, the impact of this was limited.

Ruling classes always tend to believe in the power of their own propaganda, and our current rulers are particularly prone to hubris. The *Financial Times'* Wolfgang Münchau recently compared the behaviour of today's elites to the French Bourbon monarchy who failed to pick up signs of terminal discontent and blundered on into revolution. 'The Bourbons,' he writes, 'were hard to beat as the quintessential out of touch establishment. They have competition now.'[3] The British elite has got richer quicker than almost any in the world, and they are more remote from the wider population than at any time since the 1920s. No wonder they are stunned by current developments.

Shock amongst the liberal intelligentsia needs a bit more explanation. While the advocates of the neoliberal order have failed to convince the population at large, one of the defining stories of the last 40 years has been the construction of a new political 'centre' around the anti-ideology of the free market. This has involved a growing convergence between notions of liberalism and free market prejudices. The pivotal event in this process was the neoliberals' capture of the Labour Party. Blair's 1997 election victory was an intensely contradictory moment. It marked the point at which the wider population publicly rejected Thatcherism but also the moment when social democracy fully capitulated to the market and when large sections of the liberal middle classes acclimatised themselves to the new world order.

Progressive taxation, nationalisation, and welfarism, all of which had long had some support amongst sections of the middle class could now be dismissed as passé. Labour itself had finally accepted they were outdated and that properly overseen, the market could be made to work for all. The fuzzily progressive rhetoric of the Third Way helped facilitate this, but it was also helped by the fact that all sorts of senior professionals were on the winning side of the economic divisions in a more and more divided society. While much 'professional' work has been routinized over the last few decades, people at the top of the professions have seen huge boosts to their income. Taken together, these trends forged a 'liberal' establishment that not only finds it hard to comprehend the experience of the majority of society, but has largely internalised the values of the regime. Collectivism has never sat comfortably with liberal attitudes, but recently some sections of the liberal elite have learnt an open contempt for ideas that challenge the status quo. They have also developed a habit of dressing reactionary attitudes in a cheapened language of enlightenment values. Militant secularism, human rights, even the rhetoric of women's liberation have been deployed recently to marginalise oppressed groups, justify foreign wars and undermine the left.

The possible in the present
As a result, most commentators failed to link the series of shocks to the system with accumulated resentment at the economic regime, preferring to understand them as unconnected events or as expressions of a breakdown of civilised discourse. Looking

around the world it hardly needs to be said that regressive outcomes are a looming potential. But it has been obvious for a long time that this is not the only way things can go. Ever since the great wave of anti-capitalist protests that began in Seattle in 1999 there have been cycles of radical opposition to neoliberalism in many different parts of the world. Almost everywhere there have been mass demonstrations, direct action and major strikes, in some countries real popular insurgences and even revolutionary upheavals. More recently, in Europe and elsewhere, radical political opposition has re-emerged as new left parties have begun to challenge the old order. Joining parties, which sociologists were telling us a few years ago was a dying habit, is now all the rage and, in Britain, it is parties of the left that people are choosing. Labour under Jeremy Corbyn is the biggest political party in Europe, and it is his radical challenge to the politics of war and neoliberalism that has got it to the top spot.

The emergence of political alternatives from mass movements has become a feature of radical politics over the last few decades. It has played out, with local variations, from Venezuala and Bolivia to Italy, Spain, Greece and France. Corbyn himself is an insurgent outsider whose popularity originates in his record in the protest movements. But Britain is unique, at least in Europe, in that popular anger is expressing itself through a challenge to the old regime in social democracy instead of bypassing the old centre-left parties as it has in Greece, Spain, France and elsewhere. This has catapulted radical politics to centre stage in Britain, but it comes with problems. The internal battle over Labour's direction has created enormous confusion, and attempted sabotage by the right in Labour must have significantly reduced its vote. It is a battle that is far from over.

Class and condescension

The resulting turmoil has many possible outcomes. But we

need to keep in mind that the source of the crisis lies in the gathering failure of the ruling economic and political regime and a growing popular rebellion against it. This means that the left has huge opportunities, though this is not how the left itself always sees it. There is sense of anxiety, and sometimes even resignation, amongst some opponents of neoliberalism. Partly this is a product of historic defeats and setbacks, but it is also linked to a tendency to buy into the elites self-belief, to accept their take on what 'ordinary people' think and therefore overestimate neoliberalism's popular appeal and its ideological influence. This has a long pedigree, particularly amongst left commentators with little actual contact with working people and their organisations. In the 1980s a series of widely read articles and papers published mostly in the journal *Marxism Today* judged that Thatcherism marked a new stage in capitalism's ability to incorporate working people and undermine collective aspirations.[4] Such thoughts have long been influential on the academic left, but they haven't been confined to the universities or the radical left. Kinnock's Labour leadership in the 1980s drew on them to make a public argument that a decisive ideological victory had been achieved by the right. One conclusion was that the right-wing media was unchallengeable and that a deal had to be made with them. 'If you can't beat them, join them' became a siren call of submission not just to the Murdoch press but to everything it stood for. It amounted to the internalisation of Thatcher's mantra that 'there is no alternative'.[5]

A strong sense of the elite's ideological power has continued to influence the left's analysis. Just over a decade ago, Frederic Jameson, one of modern capitalism's most searing and sophisticated critics, articulated a widespread sense of the system's invincibility, describing it as 'a locked social geology so massive that no visions of modification seem possible'.[6] This was after a wave of popular anti-capitalist struggles had hit the streets and the headlines and a massive global anti-war movement had blocked the centres of many of the world's capitals. Such a suffocating take on late capitalism's powers of social control encourages passivity, if not despair. But strong views of power can do deeper damage. In the 1980s, the worry that workers had bought into the regime morphed into a belief that class was no longer a useful category. Nowadays commentators of all sorts routinely downplay class and write off the prospect of working-class resistance. Rumours of the death of the working class have in fact been exaggerated. Not only do the overwhelming majority of British people have to work for a living, most self-define as working-class. Not only is there a growing class-based anger in British society but there is still a strong tradition of working-class organisation and a recent history of militant and powerful mass movements.

The downplaying of class and class experience contributes to a sense of melancholy not just because it obscures the main points of resistance in society, but also because it misses the main source of radical, oppositional ideas. The great intellectual achievements of left-wing politics have always been closely tied to mass movements. Marx insisted that his role was not, like the utopian socialists before him, to reimagine the world, but to draw out the potential in the existing one. The importance of the working class for Marx was that its strategic location at capitalism's heart gave it not just an unparalleled power to disrupt the system and an interest in challenging it, but also privileged access to understanding it. It was precisely the rootedness of his ideas in the real experience of this class with 'radical chains' that confirmed for Marx the validity, the 'this sidedness' as he put it, of his thought.[7]

The left needs new thinking, but it must be based on a creative recapture of some insights that should never have been relinquished in the first place. It is not just that capitalism is a deeply divisive system that benefits a tiny minority of the population, or that it impoverishes working people as a matter of course. It is a system that creates a social force with an interest in defeating it. Some talk of the need for the emergence of a new 'radical subject' to challenge the system. But the radical subject is already there, and it isn't only a slumbering, passive potential. There are millions of real, active people in communities, workforces and colleges who are more and more enraged by the experience of actually existing capitalism. Amongst them there are already networks of hundreds of thousands of students and young people, trade unionists and political campaigners trying to make sense of the situation and organise to take on an economic order that is running into the ground. The following pages take a longer look at how we got to where we are as a contribution to the discussion about how best these networks of resistance can shape the future.

The storm they call progress

The brief history of the imposition of neoliberalism on British society in the next chapter shows that, while the elites were persuaded of the need for a new economic course by the end of the 1970s, what followed was a messy and traumatic imposition of the model on a militant working class. The result was, amongst other things, massive and well supported resistance, including some of the longest strikes in labour movement history anywhere. There were moments when the new regime's advance could have been reversed. Resistance was overcome, partly due to a series of accidents, mainly due to organisational and political weakness on the side of those resisting. Right-wing splits from Labour, the rightward trajectory of the Labour leadership and ultimately insufficient solidarity were more important to neoliberalism's staying power than any process of mass persuasion.

Chapter 2 describes the crystallisation of the neoliberal centre and the forces that have led to its fracture. Blairism's 'cool Britannia' moment was brief but important. The Iraq catastrophe and the essential economic continuity of the Third Way disillusioned many 'traditional' Labour voters by 2005. But by this time, Blair's pro-market faction had secured the party machine and helped normalise free market ideas across much of the professional elite under a thin veneer of socially progressive ideas. The resulting regime only accelerated alienation from mainstream politics. Chapter 3 brings the story up to date by examining the evidence of today's social attitudes. A host of studies and surveys record a post-crash radicalisation and a growing anger at inequality, austerity and corruption in public life. It is these moods which are driving the current turmoil. They are being bent and twisted by existing institutions, but they are also helping to destabilise the structures of power. What has followed is a complex crisis of democracy that is being obscured rather than clarified by most mainstream analysis.

Conventional accounts of how public opinion is formed can't process these kinds of developments, and relying on them helped to conceal the gathering storm. Chapter 4 challenges the myth of Middle England but argues that more radical takes on ideology are also flawed. In particular, they tend to stress the power of propaganda without recognising the way that lived experience can generate opposition. There is a critical Marxist tradition that is sensitive both to the fracturing and mystifying aspects of the experience of capitalism and its tendency to store up rebellion. This is a tradition we need now more than ever. Chapter 5 makes the case that while working life is being transformed by new technologies, new industries and new working practices, class is making a comeback. The much referenced 'white working class' is a fiction partly conjured up to stop us thinking about today's multi-ethnic, gender mixed workforce as a potentially cohesive radical force. That long process of cohesion is above all, of course, a practical one, and the chapter goes on to suggest that it may not take the same forms as it has in the past. Important research backs activist experience in showing that the last two decades have seen a marked increase in political protest which has drawn together hundreds of thousands of mainly working-class activists into new networks and movements.

Despite popular opposition and despite the Corbyn surge, the British ruling class remains addicted to a toxic cocktail of free trade, financialisation and militarism, to drastically shrinking a welfare system it once tolerated and to spreading the insecurity on which its profits now depend. So it remains on a collision course with a working population less and less prepared to tolerate the intolerable. The fightback has begun in earnest. The final chapter suggests that it is high time to abandon awe of the neoliberal elites. The left must not baulk at the scale of the task ahead, or stand on the side lines composing 'correct' programmes and propaganda. But nor can we simply rely on the new politics of a re-energised Labour party, however welcome they are. The establishment may have been knocked off balance, but it has immense resources to draw on. Its recent behaviour may have been erratic, but it has also been ruthless. To prevail, we are going to have to radically strengthen our own resources, intellectually and organisationally.

1

We Never Bought the Dream

The working class is instinctively, spontaneously social democratic.
Vladimir Lenin[1]

At the end of the 1980s events had come together to create a moment of triumphalism for the Western ruling classes. During the decade, in the USA, Britain and elsewhere, governments and employers had won a series of decisive battles against organised workers. Humiliation in these high profile conflicts sapped workers' enthusiasm for resistance and cleared the way for the dismantling of large parts of the welfare state. Private capital bought out nationalised industries at knockdown rates. Union busting, privatisation and restructuring ripped through society, restoring profit rates, if not productivity. Internationally, a debt crisis had landed a tranche of developing world economies in the laps of the Western banks. At the end of the decade economic failure and discontent led to the collapse of the Eastern European satellites of the USSR. The meltdown of the Soviet Union's state-run economy was clearly imminent.

It was possible to announce a historic victory for the forces of the free market – and the Western democratic model that was apparently its purest political incarnation. When, in a 1989 essay, American political scientist Francis Fukuyama announced the 'end of history', he wasn't saying that nothing more would happen in the world. He was claiming liberal democracy as the 'final form of human government'. 'At the end of history,' he wrote, 'it is not necessary that all societies become successful liberal societies, merely that they end their ideological pretensions of representing different and higher forms of human society'.[2]

This triumphalism had a profound effect on intellectual life. The victory of an economic paradigm was judged to have buried alternatives and ushered in a world beyond ideology in which reason and the free market had synchronised. American commentator and historian Thomas Frank noted that, for some, the free market came to define what it meant to be human:

> Only when people act within the marketplace, such thinkers told us, do they act rationally, chose rightly and make their own wishes known transparently. Only then could business give us what we wanted, cater to our freely expressed choices. Markets are where we are most fully human; markets are where we show that we have a soul. To protest against markets is to surrender one's very personhood, to put oneself outside the family of mankind.[3]

Outriding

Britain was an early adopter. Margaret Thatcher, prime minister from 1979 to 1991, was one of the great champions of the free market economics that became known as neoliberalism. At its heart initially was a tight monetary policy to counter rising inflation, antipathy to the 'nanny state' and a deep hostility to working-class organisation. But it evolved into an assault on all the ways that the state had accommodated the demands of working people since World War Two and on the manufacturing base of British capitalism. Rhetorically, Thatcher went one better than Fukuyama, claiming in an interview with *Woman's Own* two years before the latter's end of history moment that 'there is no such thing as society', just 'individual men and women and their families'.[4] The aim clearly was to discredit collective organisation and ideas, but the guiding thought was that they had been made redundant in a post-ideological world. The impersonal mechanisms of the market were delivering an ideal end-state for human civilisation.

Faced with retreat and rollback on what felt like every front, some of the left internalised this onslaught. In particular, a group of influential intellectuals around the journal *Marxism Today* popularised the idea of 'new times'. They gave ground to the free market lobby by arguing that capitalism had indeed entered a new phase in which consumerism dominated so effectively it was dissolving class identities. The right had seen the future and run with it, the left had to adapt or die. In the words of one such essay from 1988:

> For more and more people it is outside work, outside the formal political structures, in the world of holidays, home interiors and superstores, that they have a sense of power and freedom to express themselves, to define their sense of self, to mould the good life. Thatcherism has not created that scenario, but the current present political culture has certainly capitalised on it. On the current climate the invitation is to 'buy out of politics', to see it only as to do with restrictive bureaucracy and petty nuisance. Life it seems, lies elsewhere.[5]

In the memorable words of the most notable proponent of 'new times', Stuart Hall, 'capital' was marching 'simultaneously across the globe and through the Maginot Lines of our subjectivities'.[6] The sense that the logic of commodity had invaded every aspect of our lives, influencing our behaviour and colonising the way we think and feel, remains influential on the left 30 years later. In his 2010 account of the neoliberals' coming to power, Jamie Peck's starting point is that:

> The conventional wisdom can seem ubiquitous, inevitable, natural, and all-encompassing. To many, neoliberalism has become practically indistinguishable from the alleged "logic" of globalization – it seems to be everywhere, and it

seems to be all that there is.[7]

The tale of how ideological 'outriders' successfully promoted the neoliberal creed in the corridors of power has been well told recently.[8] Conversion wasn't automatic even amongst the elites; as late as the mid-1980s Margaret Thatcher was still fighting a war against 'the wets', so-called 'One Nation' Tories concerned about the political and social costs of the new model. But the story of neoliberalism's roll-out in wider society is much more about imposition and confrontation than persuasion or incorporation. This story, combined with evidence about popular attitudes at the time, casts doubt on the idea of neoliberal capitalism's total ideological victory. It suggests that the paradigm, in fact, prevailed through a combination of a state strategy of class struggle, some good fortune for Thatcher and her supporters and shortcomings on the part of the opposition.

Labour and the damage done

The British ruling class adopted the new economics piecemeal and pragmatically as a result of the failure of the existing model. A broad social radicalisation at the end of World War Two had eventually forced a cross-party consensus that a mixed economy combining elements of state and private ownership was necessary for economic development. As Britain moved into the long boom, it was possible to meet some working-class aspirations through public spending on housing, health and welfare. But growth rates started to decline at the end of the 1960s, and slumped in the 1970s. For a time, governments met workers' continuing demands by printing additional money, not yet covered by the real economy. They ran into problems in the early 1970s. Inflation more than doubled to 24.6% between 1973 and 1975, and unemployment reached a million by 1975.[9] From the point of view of the capitalist class, inflation was the result of wage demands that couldn't be paid for by current levels of profit.

The slowdown in growth was international, the product of an end of the effects of huge levels of arms spending which had offset a long-term decline in profits. But Britain's economic performance was exceptionally poor, due to low levels of investment and a resulting slide in productivity. As a contemporary economist explained, 'whereas in 1870 Britain enjoyed the highest productivity amongst the major capitalist economies, by 1970, it had one of the lowest'.[10] The turn towards tight money and cutbacks was in fact instigated by Labour. In the words of *Financial Times* journalist, Peter Riddell, 'If there has been a Thatcher experiment, it was launched by Denis Healey'.[11] Healey was the chancellor in the 1974–9 Labour government which, despite promises of state intervention and redistribution, cut public spending by 9.5% from 1976 to 1978. This was far more draconian than anything Thatcher managed.[12] At Labour's conference in 1976, prime minister Callaghan dramatically renounced the Keynesian project:

We used to think you could spend your way out of a recession, and increase employment by cutting taxes and boosting government spending. I tell you in all candour that option no longer exists, and that in so far as it ever did exist, it only worked on each occasion since the war by injecting a bigger dose of inflation into the economy, followed by a higher level of unemployment.[13]

The Labour government then proceeded to negotiate an incomes policy that had a devastating impact on workers' living standards. In 1977 an *Observer* economist commented:

The past twelve months have almost certainly seen the sharpest fall in real living standards of Britain's working population in any year for at least a century, including the wars. Indeed to find a comparable fall, it will probably be necessary to go back to the eighteenth or early nineteenth centuries.[14]

The Callaghan government was able to do this because of its close relations with the trade union leaders. Union leaders were all committed to Labourism, and when faced with a Labour government in economic trouble, they could see no alternative but to help bail it out. And the impact of Labourism on workers' organisation ran deeper. The shop stewards' networks that had helped organise industrial struggle strong enough to bring down the previous Tory government were drawn into a strategy of industrial participation. This involved collaborating with management, state and private, and it removed many of them from the shop floor, making them more open to the perspectives of the boardroom. The key structures of the trade unions failed to defy the logic of retrenchment.[15]

But if much of the official labour movement reluctantly accepted the need for restraint, the rank and file would not. In 1979, after three years of punishing pay cuts, ordinary trade unionists rebelled in what came to be called the 'winter of discontent'. Local government workers and lorry drivers led the way with indefinite action in a massive wave of strikes. There were more strike days 'lost' in 1979 than at the height of the anti-Tory resistance in 1972.[16] The country was brought to a virtual standstill. But despite this inspirational self-activity, the context was very different from the heady days of the early 1970s. Labour's capitulation to market logic and its failure to meet aspirations for change had created uncertainty and demoralisation across the board. Some of the radical left effectively supported Labour's line, and influenced networks of solidarity already weakened by participation and sectionalism. The left and the movement reached an impasse that couldn't be overcome by straightforward trade union militancy.

Force and fraud

This was the situation that Margaret Thatcher brilliantly exploited to win the 1979 election. Given Labour had accepted the logic of a tight fiscal policy and attacks on workers' living standards, it was possible for the new leader of the Tory Party to blame the strikers for the chaos and Labour for going soft on them. But exploiting a difficult moment for the Labour movement was not the same as winning consent for an all-out onslaught on the working class. The cutbacks that she introduced on gaining office were mild by her later standards, but they generated deep opposition. By 1981, polls showed that she was running the most unpopular government since records began, with an approval rating of just 16%.[17] Across Britain, a cycle of riots expressed anger at the police and outrage at the damage inflicted on urban communities by the new regime.

A number of things saved her. First, Labour was sabotaged by a right-wing split from the party. Four leading MPs quit the party in 1981, claiming it was too left wing, and formed the so-called Social Democratic Party. This fatally split the anti-Tory vote in the 1983 and 1987 elections. In the 12 months of internecine warfare that followed the split, Labour's polling halved from 47.5% to 23.5%.[18] Second, Thatcher was assisted in the 1983 election by whipping up jingoism around the Falklands War. More generally, Thatcher's privatisations, the destruction of swathes of industry and her ideological aggression had a demoralising impact on organised workers already reeling from the experience of the Labour government. Cheap council house sell offs and a series of bargain basement share offers lent some short term credibility to her free market bluster. By 1987, voter turnout had started to decline and in that year's election, 60% of trade unionists voted for someone other than Labour.[19] As one historian of the Tory Party put it:

Thatcher didn't win elections because she won a majority

of people to her cause (she didn't) or because she was personally popular (she wasn't). She delivered them because her governments delivered just enough tangible benefits to just enough voters at just the right time in order to defeat an opposition whose record was woeful.[20]

But none of this could have happened without two other things. The first was a conscious and coordinated assault on the organised working class aimed at eradicating its fighting spirit, breaking up its organisation and proving by example that resistance was futile. The strategy had been planned during the years of opposition. Its architect, Sir Nicholas Ridley, recommended picking well-prepared confrontations with key groups of workers while criminalising all forms of solidarity. The set piece of the 'Ridley Plan' was the confrontation with the coal miners that began with the Coal Board's provocative closure of 20 pits in March 1984. The government had prepared by stockpiling coal, reorganising the police force and mobilising *agents provocateurs* and high level surveillance. Energy Secretary Nigel Lawson compared the operation to 're-arming to face the threat of Hitler in the 1930s'.[21]

The Great Miners' Strike was the longest major strike in European history and involved heroic levels of organisation and solidarity. It was hugely popular amongst most workers precisely because it was seen as a struggle against Thatcher's government and everything it stood for. Trade unionists and socialists organised support groups in every corner of the country, which collected huge amounts of money, food and other essentials to sustain the strikers. There were times during the dispute when Thatcher felt the government might lose the strike, in particular during the summer of 1984, when it looked as if the dockers might open up a second front.[22] Defeat was sealed by the failure of the working-class movement to turn the mood of solidarity into effective action, despite the best efforts of thousands of activists. The Labour leadership never supported the strike and did everything it could to undermine support and distance itself from the strike. The leaders of the trade unions never defied the ban on solidarity action, and the left and the rank and file were not able to deliver sufficient action independently. A devastating defeat, the miners' strike was followed swiftly by assaults on other key groups of organised workers, in particular the printers at Rupert Murdoch's News International. Once again resistance was impressive. The printers struck against new technology and massive redundancies for 54 weeks, and the movement mounted a series of big marches, protests and pickets at Murdoch's new Wapping plant. But once again, practical solidarity never reached the levels necessary to turn the tables on a more and more confident employing class.

Fantasy realism

The second crucial component in Thatcher's success was the Labour leadership's embrace of some of her pet ideas. By the second half of the decade the Labour leadership under Neil Kinnock was in full ideological flight, not just distancing itself from any kind of trade union resistance, but ditching support for nationalisation and increased public spending. Kinnock and his coterie were learning to love the free market. In the run-up to the 1987 election, Brian Gould, campaign manager and guru of the new turn, was arguing 'the idea of owning shares is catching on, and as socialists we should support it as one means of taking power from the hands of the few and spreading it more widely', and in a key document for the election 'New jobs for Britain' Kinnock himself wrote:

> We need a workforce that wants to be on the winning side, but we also need those who can manage – and manage to make it all work... the days of 'Them' and 'Us' are gone now. We are in all this together, and it is only together that Britain

will make its way in the world.[23]

One after the other, policies that contradicted the new economics were dropped. Signals were sent that Labour would be business friendly, that it would prioritise fighting inflation and even accept some of Thatcher's anti-union laws. The *Financial Times* saw the significance of this move in particular:

> Never before has the Labour Party, created by the unions, attempted to bring in controls of trade union activities on the scale proposed... Never before has Labour tried to make that control statutory, backing it up – albeit in modified form – with the involvement of the courts, traditionally seen within the Labour movement as the enemy.[24]

The retreat of some of the rest of the left helped smooth Labour's path. *Marxism Today's* 'New Times' series arguing that Thatcher's triumph represented a new, popular phase of capitalism had a real impact. The idea that share ownership had transformed capitalism's ability to share wealth, that consumption rather than production had become the defining feature of the system and 'traditional' categories of class no longer applied, became commonplace. Kinnock demonstrated the penetration of these ideas into the labour movement in his 1987 speech to the Labour Party when he quoted union leader Ron Todd:

> What do you say to a docker who earns £400 a week, owns his own house, a new car, microwave and video as well as a small place near Marbella? You do not say – let me take you out of your misery brother.[25]

Never mind that in reality the average wage of a male manual worker was £163.60 a week, or that grade one dockers in East London earned a basic rate of £181. In the Labour Party and amongst trade union leaders the need for a 'new realism' seemed self-evident. Leaving aside income levels, the sea change they identified in popular attitudes was largely imaginary. Opinion polls and attitude surveys show a stubborn collectivism and attachment to the welfare state, particularly amongst working people, right through the 1980s and the 1990s. As leading pollster John Curtice argued in his research into public opinion in 1987, 'The Thatcher revolution has simply not so far been accompanied by an equivalent revolution in public attitudes'. In fact, polls showed that in that very year, more than three quarters of the population thought 'the nation's wealth is shared unfairly', 54% that 'big business benefits owners at the expense of workers' and 59% that 'there is one law for the rich and another for the poor'. As Curtice concluded, 'within the working class there is a large majority with radical or egalitarian views'.[26]

The price of retreat

The fundamental problem was not that Thatcher's ideas had won hearts and minds, but that opposition had not broken through. The impact of the defeat of successive workers' struggles sapped people's fighting spirit and in the process weakened belief in the practical possibility of alternatives. The miners' strike, the crucial struggle of the decade, had a palpable impact on polling. At the height of the strike, Labour was ahead in the polls. As the government regained the initiative towards the end of 1984, Labour support slumped by more than 10%. A downward spiral of demoralisation followed. The government's attempt to break workers' resistance was eased by the Labour leadership's refusal to back any struggles. Defeats in turn reinforced Labour's shift rightwards. The 1987 election failure was used to justify further retreat. This was disastrous. The number of people who believed there was a good deal of difference between the major political parties plummeted from 82% in 1987 to 55% in 1992 and then down to 32% in 1997.[27] This was the background to

Kinnock's 1992 election defeat, a shocking result just months after Thatcher had been forced to resign and at a time when the Tories were in turmoil over their attitude to the European Single Market.

Despite these setbacks, and completely counter to the thinking that dominated the mainstream left, polls and surveys show a growth in left-wing attitudes throughout the period. The number of people supporting increased spending to end poverty and to bolster the NHS, and the number of people who supported nationalisation and opposed privatisation all rose between 1979 and 1992, and rose again between 1992 and 1997.[28] Polls showed too the sense that the rich were too powerful was growing. Meanwhile confidence in key institutions, including the police, the media and the banks, was well into their long slide.[29] What is more, in the real world, struggle continued in the 1990s. Thatcher's political demise was more than anything the product of the popular resistance to the hated Poll Tax. This struggle involved a mass non-payment campaign and culminated in a 250,000-strong London demonstration that turned into a riot after it was attacked by the police. Labour failed to benefit from the popular revulsion with the tax because it consistently distanced itself from the struggle. Leader Neil Kinnock denounced the protesters as 'toy town revolutionaries', Labour's shadow home secretary, Roy Hattersley, urged police to arrest rioters, and Labour councils were responsible for the imprisonment of two-thirds of those jailed.[30]

In the months after the 1992 fiasco there was another outburst of working-class struggle, this time in response to the Tories' decision to shut 31 more coal mines, effectively bringing an end to mining as a major industry. Two enormous demonstrations within a few days brought a quarter of a million people into the streets. Labour and the TUC leadership between them frittered away the chance of an effective fightback, but from this moment on, Labour started climbing in the polls. A modest increase in strike activity, Labour's steadily improving polls and the growth in Labour's membership, were all witness to a growing left-wing mood through the early 1990s. The accumulated experience of the neoliberal regime, the Tory shambles and the experience of mass mobilisations had fostered a slow return of confidence. But if Thatcher had ultimately failed to convince the British people, she was an astute class warrior to the end. When asked years later what was her greatest achievement, she replied, 'Tony Blair and New Labour'.[31]

2

The Second Death of Liberal England

I always thought my job was to build on some of the things she had done rather than reverse them.

Tony Blair on Margaret Thatcher[1]

The collapse of the centre ground of politics is widely mourned. We are being asked to believe that it threatens pluralist politics, the democratic process, even rational thought.[2] But today's centrist politics is a creature of the neoliberal onslaught. It is a product of the conflation of ideas of freedom and liberty, even democracy, with the rigours of the free market. If Thatcher never won the hearts and minds of the majority, she played an important role in spreading neoliberal ideas amongst the elites. A North Atlantic curiosity when she came to power, by the end of her tenure, variants of neoliberalism were being pursued by the majority of the world's ruling classes. In Britain, elite acceptance of neoliberal economics was early and unusually complete. The common sense of the right had been realigned by the early-1980s and a consensus was secured that the welfare state was a problem, and that if the market was allowed to rip, everyone would be better off. Although by the start of the 1990s doubts were spreading in elite circles about the wisdom of continuing a full-frontal assault on working people, everyone was satisfied that there really was no alternative to the market.

New Labour was essential to ensuring this continuity and to normalising neoliberalism. Tony Blair showed some flair in presenting his vision as a 'third way' that would make globalisation work more inclusively. In the process, New Labour crystallised a political centre that appeared socially progressive. Blair scrapped the homophobic Section 28 law and introduced civil partnerships for gay couples. He instituted a rock bottom minimum wage. His tenure coincided with a period of steady economic growth, which allowed him to increase spending on schools and the NHS, though this extra money was mostly pumped through the private sector. Initially, he managed to 'triangulate' electorally. Simply by being Labour leader he channelled the rising sense amongst working people that the Tory Party had to go. By energetic lobbying and clear signals of a radical rethink of social democratic certainties, he attracted important big business backing at a time when the Tories had run out of road. Signals were sent out from the Murdoch press and others to the middle classes that it was safe to vote Labour. The Third Way was a fantasy fusion of working-class aspiration for change with social liberalism that drew on disenchantment with the free market, while actually continuing it. For a short time, it convinced some that Britain was evolving into a meritocracy and that minor adjustments to a basically sound economic model could bring an end to the years of boom and bust.

Whatever the illusions, the extent to which the Labour leadership had surrendered to neoliberal ideas is clear from its 1997 manifesto and the book by Peter Mandelson and Roger Liddle, *The Blair Revolution: Can New Labour Deliver?* on which it was based. The strategy was 'to move forward from where Margaret Thatcher left off rather than dismantle everything she did', because 'we have to be clear where the Conservatives got things right'. The anti-union laws and privatisation were praised and renationalisation was abandoned. The 'rigour of competitive markets' was recognised, and making the market economy prosper was adopted as the key aspiration.[3] The government that followed was true to its word. Despite relatively favourable circumstances, not only was there no overturn of key Tory policies, but the programme of council house building – one of the great social democratic achievements in

Britain – was terminated as social housing was handed over to housing associations. Meanwhile, student fees were introduced and private investment brought into the NHS. In 1999, Colin Hay, an academic at the University of Birmingham, found an almost complete convergence of New Labour and Tory policies in industrial policy, education, training, pensions and crime.[4] Consequently, economic injustice continued to grow. If you glance at a chart of the rising income share of the 1% over these years, the moment of New Labour's election is imperceptible.[5]

Despite some initial enthusiasm, once it was rolled out, the programme was never tremendously popular. It is widely known that Labour haemorrhaged nearly a million votes in Blair's third election in 2005, largely as a result of the travesty of the Iraq War. But in Blair's second election in 2001, Labour's vote was also not just dramatically down on 1997, it was three quarters of a million down on 1992, the year Neil Kinnock lost so disastrously to the Tories. The political damage was limited because the convergence of the parties was generating cynicism and indifference toward mainstream politics. Between 1997 and 2001, turnout dropped from 71.5% of the electorate to 59.1%, the second lowest figure since the popular vote was won.[6] New Labour's programme was more than anything a reflection of the views of key sections of the British ruling class. Peter Mandelson's team were famously in close touch with the '17 people who count in Britain', almost all of them leading figures from business and finance. The taskforces that Tony Blair set up to supervise industries and services were packed full of leading figures from banks, big business and trade associations.[7] But Blair's rhetoric, scattering of progressive social policies and skilful repackaging of neoliberal values had helped legitimise neoliberalism across important sections of the middle classes.

Money talks

Neoliberalism's ability to cohere a workable social alliance, including support in professional circles beyond the Tory middle-class bastions, depended also on its one unambiguous economic achievement: an enormous shift in wealth from the poor to the rich. Until Thatcher, the share of income received by the richest 1% in Britain had been declining steadily since before World War One. Between 1920 and 1979 it fell from over 16% to 4% after tax. By the time Thatcher left office it was back up to over 8%.[8] Comparisons between the fortunes of the bottom 10% and those in the top show sharp shifts in the Thatcher years. But the trend continued after her. By the mid-2000s, Britain was one of the most unequal societies in the developed world, lagging behind only the USA, Italy and Portugal amongst so-called advanced countries.[9]

Remarkably, the economic crisis of 2008 hasn't slowed the process. Britain's inequality is growing as fast as any in the world and it is on course to become the most unequal of the richest 25 countries. Wealth inequality grows exponentially towards the top of the scale. The richest thousand saw their wealth double between 2005 and 2015 to an average of more than half a billion. A good way beneath them, but still undeniably thriving, is a growing layer of senior management, top civil servants and professionals who have made it into the 1%.[10] Their fortunes have improved so dramatically that even the right-wing press from time to time feels the need to complain about their lavish lifestyles. *The Daily Telegraph* has claimed that more than 700 'civil servants, officials and quangocrats' now earn more than £100,000 a year. Many earn much, much more. One culprit picked out by the *Telegraph* is Simon Kirby, the chief executive of railway project High Speed 2, who is paid a basic annual salary of £750,000.[11] Neoliberalism has been kind to senior managers, top professionals and all sorts of 'opinion formers', helping to ensure that strategic institutions in industry, academia, the civil service and the media overlook the glaring injustice at neoliberalism's heart. As Danny Dorling has brilliantly explained, growing wealth inequality has wider implications, including a social segregation that ensures that elites live more and more remotely from the wider population:

> From the late 1970s onwards, actual salaries at the top end began to diverge upwards rapidly. Warped morals also began to be countenanced again in countries like Britain, morals that suggested that competition was good, cooperation bad, just a few were truly talented and that they should have their talents supposedly 'justly rewarded'. If you begin to believe that, you became more and more careful who you slept with. It was not just that the lives of the rich became more separated from the lives of the poor, but that the implications of mixing became more daunting... Income inequalities rose, and as they rose the idea of mixing socially with those a little well-off became just a little less palatable with every year that passed.[12]

Accumulating discontent

What the newly wealthy fatally fail to understand of course, is that the up flow of wealth that has helped legitimise neoliberalism in polite circles has had the opposite effect in the wider world. This is the secret to the current shock and confusion in the mainstream. It is not that some people have been left behind, as commentators rather patronisingly put it. Nor is it a question simply of the growth of relative poverty, bad enough though that would be. Data collected under the 2010 coalition government shows that *living standards continued to fall for all but the very rich*.[13] This, of course, is no accident. Any honest analysis of the way neoliberal capitalism works has to conclude that its ability to increase the wealth of the elites *depends* on making working people poorer. The much promised moment when all the sacrifice will lead to wider prosperity is constantly deferred. In less guarded moments, it is completely forgotten. Thatcher's economic advisor Alan Budd later admitted that 'the 1980s policies of attacking inflation by squeezing the economy and public spending were a cover to bash the workers'; the aim was a low wage, privatised economy wide open to foreign investment.[14] The results continue to be devastating. Neoliberalism's success as a class strategy has necessarily been experienced as regression by the majority and as a catastrophe for large numbers at the bottom. The numbers living on less than median income are rising, leading to an increase in a host of different forms of deprivation. Almost half the population cannot afford to replace a fridge or cooker immediately if it breaks down, while levels of homelessness and mental health problems are spiralling.[15] Until the late 1970s, most working-class people felt that they were better off than their parents and that probably their children would be better off than them. Now the majority of society believes, rightly, that it is becoming worse off. And people expect things to get worse, not better, as they get older and as their children grow up. How could anyone believe this was not going to change attitudes to society on a monumental scale?

Just measuring income changes fails to capture the full impact of the neoliberal assault. The programme of privatisation at its core, while opening up swathes of previously nationalised life to private capital accumulation, has further impoverished people's lives by decimating social services that people now have to pay for or do without. This kind of 'accumulation by dispossession' is class struggle economics at its most brazenly public and political. At the same time as increasing the well of misery in society it has had a huge ideological impact. As David Harvey argued more than ten years ago, it has generated resistance and provided important popular rallying points:

The corporatization and privatization of hitherto public assets (like universities) to say nothing of the wave of privatization of water and other public utilities that has swept the world, constitute a new wave of 'enclosing the commons'. As in the past, the power of the state is frequently used to force such processes through even against the popular will. As also happened in the past, these processes of dispossession are provoking widespread resistance and this now forms the core of what the anti-globalization movement is about. The reversion to the private domain of common property rights won through past class struggles (the right to a state pension, to welfare, or to national health care) has been one of the most egregious of all policies of dispossession pursued in the name of neo-liberal orthodoxy.[16]

Meanwhile, the increasingly close relations that privatisation has encouraged between big business and the state have helped to poison political life. Thatcher, it has been said, may have idolised her hard working lower middle-class father, but she produced a society in the image of her dissolute and corrupt son.[17] The 'greed is good' philosophy she championed unleashed a frenzy of freebooting and normalised corruption and venality in public life. Sleaze has been one of the key drivers of political disaffection, as a 2004 paper by the Centre for Research into Elections and Social Trends argued:

> The fall in trust and confidence mostly occurred in the early 1990s; that is, at just the moment when the word 'sleaze' entered the regular political vocabulary in Britain. Meanwhile, our own survey work indicates that those who perceive sleaze are certainly less likely to express trust and confidence in government. For example, amongst those who think that the Labour Party 'very often' does favours for those who give the party money, only 13% trust governments to put the nation's interests first.[18]

At the same time, cynicism created by political convergence, gaping inequality and the hollowing out of public life have weakened all sorts of institutions, alliances and networks that used to work as carriers for establishment ideas and values. Until the SNP, the Greens and Labour recently bucked the trend, and with the exception of an upswing for Labour in the mid-1990s, there has been a steady decline in membership of all political parties since the 1960s. The Tory Party in particular has been decimated – declining in numbers by 300% since 1970, and now boasting an average age of around 60.[19] The Church of England, which used to be described as 'the Tory Party at prayer', has now become a haven of liberal disquiet and some of its leaders openly criticise the excesses of the free market from time to time. Political action by some lawyers, the recent revolt by the junior doctors and strikes by academics show that professional groups that used to be reliably moderate are now not just alienated but sometimes actively oppositional. The breakup of state social support and decline in local government spending can atomise and fragment communities, but it also has the effect of reducing the state's local reach and legitimacy, dangerous at a time when macro policy is so deeply discredited.

Fundamental flaws

These are the problems of the success of the neoliberal model from the point of view of its champions. But if its achievements in redistributing wealth upwards have caused problems, its economic failures have made matters dramatically worse. The sheer longevity of the neoliberal trauma and the almost universal buy-in from global elites has led some commentators to forget or discount neoliberalism's fundamental flaws and contradictions. Its supporters may have claimed to be anti-ideology, but in fact they have, at least publicly, always equated individual freedom with purchasing power, and the freeing up of markets with dynamic, profitable and expanding economies.

In its own terms Neoliberalism has not just failed, it has failed on an epic scale.

In 2006, Sir John Gieve, Deputy Governor of the Bank of England, made an unusually frank speech to an academic audience. He explained that high levels of investment were the main driver of economic progress, crucial to competitiveness, profitability and wealth creation, and then went on to admit the failure of the whole project of the previous decades to restore investment levels. Low investment during the 1970s and 1980s could be explained by the level of economic turbulence, 'yet,' he said, despite the excellent business climate more recently, 'in 2005, business investment in the UK was its lowest relative to whole economy income since 1965, when official data was first collected'. He ended his speech in perplexity:

> I confess I remain puzzled. The macro environment has never been more stable. Companies have been achieving high rates of return on their investments in the United Kingdom, and finance is readily available... It is difficult not to think that opportunities are there and in time we will see the long awaited sustained recovery in investment.[20]

His hopes were misplaced. UK investment spending remained unimpressive until the crash of 2008, when it fell through the floor. It had barely pulled back to low pre-crash levels in 2015.[21] The truth is, Britain's deep structural economic problems remain after 40 years of neoliberal shock therapy. They are partly the problems of the Western economies in general. Global growth rates have fallen every decade since the 1960s. This has led to a chronic investment problem and a seventy-fold increase in the turnover of financial institutions, as the financial sector became an alternative to investment in real production.[22]

But Britain is an extreme case. Particularly low levels of productivity and investment have meant that financial services have become more and more central to what passes for ruling-class strategy over the last few decades. Its importance grew rapidly during the 1980s as capital controls were dismantled and capital's global mobility increased. As it became clear that Thatcher's policies of privatisation and deregulation were decimating Britain's manufacturing base, the City became even more central to the British ruling classes' attempt to stave off post-imperial decline and maintain a privileged position in the world. London remains the pre-eminent international financial centre for the world economy – a function of historic commercial and power relations developed in Britain's imperial heyday, the international reach of British corporations, strength and trust in the pound and the sheer scale of its capital resources. British banks and other institutions take a cut of all the capital that passes through. This income has become vital to offsetting Britain's growing balance of payments deficit.[23]

The increasing importance of finance has brought more problems with it. The banks are orientated to international markets and have very little interest in the fortunes of the wider British economy. And as Ross McKibbin has argued, the specific qualities, or lack of them, that characterise banking have come to dominate ruling-class thinking:

> The making of money, often a great deal of it, takes place in an enclosed world where long-term consequences are not considered. There has always been some feeling of separateness in banking and finance, but it has become much more pronounced in the last twenty or thirty years... But the bankers persuaded the country's political class that they were essential and that their values and ways of doing things were socially desirable. They became even more enmeshed in the system and with them came money and the love of money.[24]

Banking has fuelled the bonfire of regulation in the economy, built up the pressure for a lax tax regime, generated huge geographic imbalance between London and the South East and much of the rest of the country and massively stimulated inequality through asset stripping, mergers and acquisitions, pension fund raids and various forms of fraud. In the process, Britain, and London in particular, has become an organising and leisure centre for the super rich, amongst them some of the most parasitical and shady operators in the world. 'Ultra-high net worth individuals' is now an official category, defined as people with more than £30 million in disposable income. London is home to more of them than any other city on the planet.[25]

The centrality of financial services in the economy also, of course, supercharged the debt boom. The City of London's internationalised, deregulated banking sector helped pioneer novel ways to respond to the generally low profitability in the system by creating new forms of fictitious capital predicated on notional future profits, or future payments on mortgages. This helped keep the economy afloat in the Blair and Brown years and met the aspirations of the population, as relatively low growth continued and the social mobilisation of public debt was no longer on the political agenda. But the City's spectacular divergence from levels of productive economic activity was obviously unsustainable. By the middle of the 2000s, leverage rates (the ratio between the banks' real assets and their liabilities) had been allowed to rise from the normal order of 5 or 6, to multiples of 50 and more.[26]

The moment of truth

The banking crisis of 2008 brought all this to a head. The rhetoric of deregulation and small state turned out to be not just empty, but in bad faith. Not only had the most unfettered market imaginable gone into freefall but the immediate response of the government was to throw vast amounts of money – our money – at the banks until they stabilised and could return to their destructive business. Confidence in the banks plummeted and outrage at bankers was so great it could be felt in parliament. In a state of some panic, the Parliamentary Commission on Banking Standards went as far as to call for some bankers to be imprisoned, commenting, 'the public have a sense that advantage has been taken of them, that bankers have received huge rewards, that some of those rewards have not been properly earned, and in some cases obtained through dishonesty, and that these huge rewards are excessive, bearing little or no relation to work done'.[27] But it wasn't just the banks. The year of the banking crisis saw trust in other institutions fall sharply and a marked change in opinion over wider social issues. Any lingering idea that free markets were neutral and efficient mechanisms around which societies should be organised had crashed with the banks. There was a growing demand for human intervention and control. As austerity followed, concern over inequality and the sense that business was taking liberties rose steadily. By 2014, one study of opinion found that:

> 80% of British adults say cutting the gap between rich and poor should be a priority – more than say the government should reduce immigration, cut the benefit bill, or change the UK's relationship with the EU. And that 82% believe the benefits from business successes mostly go to owners and bosses – while workers and society carry the cost of business failures.[28]

The report concluded, 'pay gaps and concerns about business behaviour are now embedded as mainstream political issues, with voters of all the main parties identifying them as priorities'.

The situation for the elites is worse now than it was before the banking crisis. Growth has failed to rise significantly across the

OECD countries, including Britain, while indebtedness is up. Profits, dividends and bonuses in the world of finance are back to pre-2008 levels.[29] This on the basis of the massive government bailouts and cheap money from central banks. Attempts to kick start the wider economy by quantitative easing or rock bottom interest rates have failed. Looking back now over the last 40 years, low growth and low profitability appear endemic to at least the OECD economies, with Britain amongst the weaker performers. The apparent lack of any alternative policy prescriptions adds to the impression that we are witnessing not just problems with a particular paradigm, but chronic underlying weaknesses in Western capitalism itself. In Tony Norfield's words:

> A debt crisis is not really a crisis of debt, but more a sign that the economy's production of value can no longer support the previous illusion of wealth. The chronic nature of the current crisis, with persistently low rates of growth compared to earlier decades, is another sign the game is up.[30]

Post-crash, the crisis has engulfed the state. In some countries like Iceland, Ireland, Greece and Italy, it has led the state to the brink of meltdown. Elsewhere, including in Britain, the combination of bank bailouts and social cuts has drained legitimacy from established politics. Meanwhile all European business elites are terrified that the strategy of bailouts and cheap money is finished. If there was another major bank failure, central banks simply wouldn't have the resources to respond. This is the impasse in which the establishment is floundering. It is also a part of the background to the crisis over the EU.

A further impact of the banking crisis is a sharp increase in the role of supranational institutions in supervising parts of the world system and disciplining chaotic markets and 'spendthrift' governments. The increased strategic importance of the EU is one instance of this tendency for international organisations to assume some of the nation state's traditional functions, in the process limiting their freedom of manoeuvre in the interests of the freedom of capital. As radical economist Wolfgang Streeck has pointed out, concerns about these institutions' unaccountability are justified:

> Citizens increasingly perceive their governments, not as their agents, but as those of other states or of international organizations, such as the IMF or the European Union, immeasurably more insulated from electoral pressure than was the traditional nation-state. In countries like Greece and Ireland, anything resembling democracy will be effectively suspended for many years; in order to behave 'responsibly', as defined by international markets and institutions, national governments will have to impose strict austerity, at the price of becoming increasingly unresponsive to their citizens.[31]

The war economy

The British establishment's return to fighting full blooded foreign wars is closely tied up with its front edge role in the neoliberal experiment. The choice to participate in a series of wars has come fairly naturally to the leaders of the world's first and biggest modern colonial power. Partly as a function of its post-colonial position, Britain has unusually large investments and strong connections around the world. As a series of Ministry of Defence security reports insist, Britain's interests abroad need defending in a more and more contested world.[32] Britain's chosen role as a bridgehead between Europe and the USA means support for the adventures of the world's greatest superpower are pretty much non-negotiable. But the wars are not simply an expression of subordination to the USA. The Chilcot Report noted that Tony Blair and his coterie ignored a series of expert warnings of the consequences of the Iraq War. But it is notable that, despite the briefings, despite massive opposition and political turmoil in the country at large as well as unease in Whitehall, there was no internal rebellion against Blair's plans. As one senior diplomat has put it, 'I am not aware of any direct or organised challenge to the basis of policy'.[33]

The core elements of the British ruling class see foreign wars as chancy but, given Britain's widely dispersed economic interests and vulnerable position in the world, on balance worth the risks. For one thing, they provide further opportunities for accumulation by dispossession at an international level. In his examination of the economic imperatives of the Iraq War, Greg Muttit has shown, for example, the extent to which British oil companies benefited. British banks also benefit directly from military interventions. As if to illustrate the tie up between the British government, the military and the banking sector, Lady Symons, the minister who negotiated many of the post-occupation deals between the Iraqi government and UK oil companies, went on to take an advisory post with a UK merchant bank that cashed in on the deals.[34] More generally, military power projection has an important persuasive function over foreign governments, encouraging them not to pursue policies that might restrict access for British investors or to make deals with competitors. Military strength also helps to secure Britain's position at the top table at the United Nations, NATO and other international institutions, helping to ensure that the policies adopted by these bodies coincide as much as possible with its interests.

If the Iraq War and the interventions that followed were broadly approved by the British elites, they have probably done more than anything to generate popular distrust. Shocking in itself, the Iraq War revealed just how low the political elite was prepared to go in support of corporate interests, including participating in systematic destruction and lying to parliament and the people. Polls show that the majority opposed the invasion of Iraq not just because they sensed it would have a disastrous impact but also because they saw it as a war for oil.[35] The establishment is now deeply concerned by widespread anti-war sentiment, and has had to amend some of its policies accordingly. But as ever it has learnt little from popular critiques. In foreign policy circles there is a denial of even the modestly stated case against the Iraq War outlined in the Chilcot Report.

The international crisis over Syria, drawing in a series of regional and international powers into a catastrophic war, illustrates in tragically graphic terms how the economic crisis is sharpening international tensions. Faced with economic decline, the Western powers, led by the USA, are more rather than less likely to use military means to confront emerging challengers. Ignoring the way in which recent wars have destabilised the world, the British foreign policy establishment remains keen on intervention and supportive of a series of murderous proxy wars. The Labour right has been doing its best to present itself as a reliable war party. As a result, largely unnoticed by the media, British forces are currently fighting in at least seven foreign theatres.[36]

Who faked it first?

The 'crisis of the centre', then, is a product of establishment buy-in to a toxic regime of immiseration at home and war abroad. It is the outcome of years of unquestioning promotion of an international neoliberal system sliding further and further into crisis. The regime is embedded across British institutions. The financial and corporate sectors have been driving the race to the bottom, but while working lives for hospital staff, most civil servants, council workers, teachers, media workers, university staff and numerous others have become almost unbearable, the leaders of 'liberal' or public sector institutions, from the university sector to the NHS, have failed to stand up or speak out against the damage being done. Instead, in many cases, they have encouraged the hollowing out of the institutions they manage by imposing business-led models of development. The 'liberal' media in particular has proved incapable of empathising with those suffering or taking seriously any critique of this brave new world. Instead it has taken to heart the illiberal idea that there is no alternative and fallen over itself to justify unjust wars and rationalise racist attitudes.

The collapse of elite authority is a product not just of its failure to take society forward but also of the gap between official rhetoric and actually existing capitalism. And here lies the dismal irony of complaints about the return of the irrational or the emergence of a 'post-truth', 'fake news' society. Politicians and the media have been making up news for years. Before, during and after the 2008 banking crisis, key facts were suppressed, including the deliberately toxic nature of much of the debt, the uselessness of regulation, the vast amounts of public money used in the bailouts and the failure to make changes after the event. Well before that in 2002/3, politicians, the intelligence services and much of the media colluded in the construction of a phoney case for war against Iraq. Some of the neocon war leaders in the US raised contempt of 'discernible reality' to the level of a principle. In 2004, Bush's chief strategist Karl Rove told a journalist that he had little time for the 'reality based community' adding that, 'That's not the way the world really works anymore...We're an empire now, and when we act, we create our own reality.'[37]

The result is that the public discourse generated by the political and media loop is more and more degraded and far-fetched. Peter Oborne captured the essence of this during the Blair years:

Very few utterances by front rank politicians have any meaning, and fewer still correspond in even a rudimentary way to the truth. The same is the case with the reports sent back to head office by political reporters once those utterances have been made. Their 'stories' are in essential respects elaborate fictions, which can only be appreciated once it is grasped that they are not an attempt to describe the truth and certainly not to inform the reader, but rather manifestations of power.[38]

No wonder that in some places reactionary demagogues have been able to channel the cynicism created by a failed political order into politics based on right wing fantasies.

To make matters worse, in the process of defending the indefensible, the elites have adopted many of the poisonous prejudices some of them now denounce in the so-called populists. The ridiculous idea that immigrants and Muslims are the greatest threats to society hasn't come from the far right fringes, it has been announced almost daily for decades in the columns of mainstream newspapers and repeated on the front benches of parliament nearly as often. Liberals in many walks of life have succumbed and signed up to ideas about the importance of 'British values', the urgency of challenging Muslim extremism and the cultural dangers of immigration. Tony Blair perfectly encapsulated this corruption of enlightenment values in his 2006 message to would-be immigrants: 'our tolerance is part of what makes Britain, Britain. So conform to it; or don't come here'.[39]

Neoliberal confidence that the markets would dovetail with democracy to deliver the good society is a distant memory. It was always a self-serving fantasy only half-believed even amongst the elites. But rather than rethinking the free market, sections of the ruling class are having second thoughts about democracy. There is concern in ruling circles that even today's hollowed out democracy is a liability. As Wolfgang Streeck warns, 'doubts remain among the profit-dependent classes as to whether democracy will, even in its emasculated contemporary version, allow for the neoliberal "structural reforms" necessary for their regime to recover'.[40]

If the crisis continues, expect some correction towards rather more brutal and direct forms of class rule. But whatever happens, despite the elites' successes in expelling democracy from the economy and their attempts to buy up the political realm, questions of popular control and democracy are back in play.

3

The Sound of Cracking

Supporters of a market economy have a very big problem; unless they address the concerns of the public they will be annihilated.
City AM[1]

If there was an abject failure to predict the recent series of rebellions, what has followed, in the mainstream at least, has been an extraordinary failure to explain. Some commentators have sheltered from reality by simply refusing underlying explanations and treating each event in isolation and ignoring signs of overall malaise. So the Scottish vote was driven by the fashion for the politics of identity, Corbynism is an unfortunate side effect of Labour's constitutional changes, a Trotskyite plot, a purist fantasy or a personality cult. The Brexit vote was simply a xenophobic response to a too lax immigration policy inflamed by 'project fear'. Others recognised a wider malfunction, but blamed it on various forms of disengaged or irrational behaviour. Talk of apathy morphed into dismay at the spread of 'post-truth politics' or the most recent favourite, the spread of populism.

Beyond belief

Evidence of a deep crisis in the British democratic system has in fact been accumulating for years. In the last decade, politicians came near the bottom of almost all lists of the trustworthy.[2] The number of people 'tending to trust' parliament fell from 50% to 20% between 1997 and 2011. In one 2009 poll, 40% of the public claimed to 'almost never' trust national government. Another survey showed UK political parties as the least trusted in Europe.[3] Unsurprisingly, people have been turning away from electoral politics. Until 2017, there had been long-term fall off in the percentage of people voting since the 1950s, with the biggest drop in the late 1990s.[4]

Commentators and academics blamed the population for opting out and for rejecting the sound advice and attitudes of the great and the good. The comforting term 'anti-politics' was duly coined and circulated. This theme is still in favour. A recent essay on fake news in the Financial Times runs under the strapline, 'we live in a time of when emotion trumps reason, misinformation circulates freely and experts are disdained.'[5] Marginally more thoughtful voices blame elite presentational skills. One hopeful globaliser writes, 'A great intellectual failure of the past two decades is the inability to offer a more nuanced account of the market economy than that contained in the mantras of "greed is good", "eat what you kill" and "shareholder value is the goal"'.[6]

But what the elites face is not a communication problem or some popular democratic disengagement but a gathering rejection of their whole system. The growing distrust with politics was linked with a steep decline in confidence in core capitalist institutions beyond Westminster. The 2012 British Social Attitudes Survey found that the percentage who believe banks are well run had dropped from 90% in 1983 to just 19% in 2012.[7] This is a precipitous fall, though perhaps unsurprising given the banks' record. But the same survey shows that the police, the press, the BBC and a raft of other state organisations have seen their credibility drop too, if not so dramatically.

Accompanying this distrust of the institutions was a sense that big business has become too powerful. This predated the economic crash. The proportion believing that business has too much power nearly doubled from 26% to 50% between 1983 and 2007.[8] As a 2008 report into lobbying by the House of Commons

Public Administration Select Committee (PASC) argued:

> There is a genuine issue of concern, widely shared and
> reflected in measures of public trust, that there is an inside
> track, largely drawn from the corporate world, who wield
> privileged access and disproportionate influence.[9]

Even before the 2015 election, more perceptive commentators
began to notice that something more focused was emerging,
something approaching a popular critique of capitalism. A 2014
poll found that 56% thought closing the inequality gap more
important than increasing wealth, while only 17% thought the
opposite. Nearly 70% supported increasing taxes for the rich
and 48% supported a 60% rate, as against 34% who opposed it.
A survey of polling concluded, 'when it comes to capitalism,
the public is to the left of every mainstream party, including
Labour. The views of Conservative MPs on capitalism are far
away from any of the public, including their own voters'.[10]
Commenting on opinion polls in an article titled 'There is Sadly
Mass Support for Nationalization and Price Controls' Alistair
Heath of *City AM* complained, 'slowly but surely, the public is
turning its back on the free market economy and re-embracing
an atavistic version of socialism, which, if implemented,
would end in tears'.[11] To the surprise of many, Ed Miliband's
Labour failed to win the 2015 election. But the Beckett report,
Labour's internal inquiry into the election, pointed to a wide
radicalisation in society. Its conclusions contradicted much of
the post-election commentary which suggested Miliband had
drifted too far to the left. 'Some of the "left-wing policies"', it
found, 'were the most popular [and] individual policies polled
well'. The report concluded that the problem was not left-wing
policies but 'the lack of a consistent, cohesive narrative'. It cited
the redistributive mansion tax in particular as a vote winner.[12]

Two connected things had been happening over the previous

years, almost unnoticed in the mainstream. On the one hand, there was a long-term growth in the number of people self-defining as left wing. According to the World Values survey this number increased in the UK from 4.7 million in 1981 to 7.3 million in 2006, with a particularly marked upswing amongst young people. More recent surveys suggest that as many as 20% of the population self-define as left wing or very left wing.[13] A 2016 survey showed that socialism is more popular than capitalism as a concept with 36% of people saying they view socialism favourably as opposed to 32% who view it unfavorably.[14] On the other hand, there was a much wider growth in support for policies normally defined as left wing from people of all political persuasions. An LSE report, 'Ideology Is in the Eye of the Beholder', found that members and supporters of all parties – excepting the Tories but including UKIP – came up with what could only be regarded as left-wing answers to general questions about the way society was working. Even the answers from Tory members and supporters placed them only slightly to the right of centre.[15]

By 2015 polls showed that big majorities supported nationalisations of key services, increased taxes for the rich and a higher minimum wage.[16] Populus found most people believed 'the government needs to be tougher on big business', and this included 50% of Tory voters. They also discovered that 'capitalism is more likely to be regarded as a force for ill than for good by the public, while MPs – particularly Conservative MPs – generally regard it as a force for good'.[17] Meanwhile, opposition to war has grown throughout the period. Even before it started, most people opposed the attack on Iraq and the popular conclusion was that it was an oil grab not a humanitarian intervention. Most of the foreign wars pursued by successive governments since have been deeply unpopular.[18] By 2014, the Ministry of Defence was in something of a panic over the general reluctance to deploy foreign troops abroad and a growing opposition to all military aggression.[19]

Passion and politics

So, rather than a rejection of politics, what was happening was a rejection of the *type* of politics and policies on offer in the mainstream up to that point. An unjust economic system was at the top of people's concerns and they were starting to link economic malfunction with a broken political system. The near-miss independence surge in Scotland in autumn 2014 was driven by a rejection of Westminster politics connected to a revolt against the austerity economics that were the only ones on offer there. Polls showed large numbers of 'yes' voters were deeply alienated by the politics on offer in parliament and saw independence as a way to re-establish control over lives that were being devastated.[21] The three most important reasons given for voting for independence were disaffection with Westminster politics, fear for the future of the NHS and 'the principle that all decisions about Scotland should be taken in Scotland'.[23]

No wonder then that when, after thirty years of suffocating political consensus, Jeremy Corbyn's leadership finally offered a UK-wide alternative to the neoliberal nightmare, the process of political disengagement went in to full reverse. Suddenly politics was not just interesting but a matter of life-changing urgency. Thousands flocked to listen to Corbyn speak up and down the country, more than two millions registered to vote, the election turn out was the highest since 1997 and participation by 18-24 year olds shot up by more than a third to 64.5%. Labour narrowly lost the election, but in seven weeks it had achieved a swing of ten per cent, the biggest since 1945. The sheer velocity of the surge showed that there was an enormous pent up demand for a challenge to the status quo, the relentless cuts, the foreign wars, the insecurity and misery of the low wage economy, and the hateful class arrogance of those who believe they are born

The Sound of Cracking

to rule over us.

Many commentators still didn't quite get it. Some tried to explain the election result as a generational revolt, others as a fall out from Brexit, some even as an expression of educational achievement. None of these analyses survived contact with the facts. While it is true there was a swing to the Tories amongst over 55s, and that there is huge enthusiasm amongst young people for the whole Corbyn project, 25 to 34 years olds and 35 to 44 year olds, already overwhelmingly pro-Labour, swung sharply further towards Labour under Corbyn.[23] The Tories made a few gains in some areas that voted leave, but so did Labour, holding onto seats in places like Halifax and Hartlepool which the Tories were confident of winning and gaining Bury North, Stockton South, Derby North, and in seats across Wales.

Of course it was a complex vote with real local and regional variations. But one of the things that puzzled many commentators was that Labour gained votes from so many sources and in so many areas. It won votes from the SNP, from UKIP, from the Greens and the LibDems, its vote went up in Wales, in the South East, in most Northern towns, as well as in Scotland, in predominantly Leave areas and in places where most people voted Remain. No one should have been perplexed by this. As a detailed breakdown of the vote in the Guardian showed, 'The Brexit effect didn't work for May,' and areas of high deprivation voted Labour.[24] Prosperity may be uneven geographically, but even in areas of economic growth there has been a great deal of suffering. London, where Labour achieved one of its biggest vote shares since 1945, is one of the most unequal areas of the country and one in which homelessness and the cost of living are out of control. A credible call for a new politics appealed to people who had suffered across the country and diminished the attraction of various other more or less anti-establishment options. Although the process of Brexit remains an important issue, despite the Tories' best efforts, the election wasn't mainly about the EU. What was really at stake in this election was the kind of society we want to live in.

Most of the all the election result marked the return of class to British politics. Taxing the rich, the NHS, state education and tuition fees were amongst the key issues and promises of nationalisation sparked hope of an end to profiteering. The election put the lie to the conventional wisdom that post Brexit politics would be dominated by right wing agenda items such as immigration and security. But it wasn't just that people focussed on bread and butter issues. One of the most striking things about the result was the high level of general politics in play. The concerted attack on Jeremy Corbyn over his refusal to promise to 'press the nuclear button' failed to worry most of the electorate, despite the fact that an ambush was staged against him on the high-profile Question Time ten days before the election. Many felt that the two appalling terrorist attacks in the election campaign would allow Theresa May to play the security card and re-establish her 'strong and stable' credentials. In the days after the attacks the media went on a rampage over Corbyn's foreign policy record. The day before the election the Sun led with a so-called expose on 'Jezza's Jihadi Comrades', the Telegraph claimed 'Corbyn Ducks Terror Challenge' and the BBC obediently followed suit with a photomontage of Jeremy Corbyn next to Osama Bin-Laden. [25]

But this didn't make much impact either. The surge to Labour continued until election day and beyond. Corbyn had responded to the dreadful attack in Manchester by calling a press conference at which he argued that Western foreign policy was one of the drivers of the spread of terrorist attacks and organization. An opinion poll days after showed that the overwhelming majority of the population agreed with him. The ORB survey found 75 per cent of people believe interventions in Iraq, Afghanistan and Libya have made atrocities on UK soil more likely.[26]

To say that mainstream commentators were shocked by the election result would be an understatement. The result confounded their deepest convictions. Most of them had joined the political class in assuming Corbyn had little appeal outside of some mythical Islington liberal elite. Partly their contempt for and lack of contact with working class people led them to believe Corbyn's ideas would never achieve popular lift off. Partly they didn't like the ideas anyway. They had spent two years dreaming up all sorts of convoluted theories to explain away the Corbyn effect. Anything would do as long as it didn't link Corbyn's gathering popularity with wider social developments. The *Guardian*'s Jonathan Freedland's riff on Corbyn 'tribalism' was typical:

> For a lot of those taking part, choosing a party leader is not about assembling a governing majority, winning power or even making a change in society. It is about identity. It is about being true to yourself. In this sense, joining the Corbyn tribe becomes something non-negotiable, or at least impregnable to routine political arguments about electability, popular appeal and the like. Those kinds of calculations are held to be cynical, because they require you to compromise something fundamental about who you are.[27]

In fact the scale and scope of Corbyn's support was, inconceivable except as an expression of deep social trends. Labour Party membership was well over 600,000 by December 2016, up from 201,000 in May 2015, making Labour the biggest party in Western Europe. Corbyn's support was high amongst first time, often younger members and people returning to the party, and it was strongest amongst working-class members.[28]

All this contradicted the attempt by the Labour right and

their media sympathisers to present the battle in Labour as one between a moderate, practical wing in touch with ordinary people and committed to winning power, and the hopeless idealists of the left in touch only with each other. Fundamentally, this was never what the turmoil in Labour was about. Some MPs had no doubt absorbed the left's pessimism, failed to spot the mood for change and bought the idea that he is unelectable. But the Blairites and many other Corbyn opponents ran a concerted and damaging campaign of subversion, sabotage and harassment from the moment Corbyn first won because they opposed his programme and his politics. They were prepared to risk damaging Labour's electoral chances to try and destroy Corbyn's leadership.

We have seen how Blair's actual programme has never been popular. In Jeremy Gilbert's words:

> This programme has involved the introduction of profit-seeking and commercial relations into as many areas of service design and delivery as possible. A mountain of polling evidence demonstrates that only a small minority of the public – and a negligible proportion of Labour voters – has ever supported any element of this programme.[29]

Despite his image as a progressive pragmatist, and his famous penchant for focus groups, Tony Blair and his entourage have in fact always put their ideology well before worries about popularity. His passionate commitment to the neocon-led war on Iraq was no aberration and his response to Corbyn's rise has been unequivocal, 'Let me make my position clear: I wouldn't want to win on an old-fashioned leftist platform. Even if I thought it was the route to victory, I wouldn't take it'.[30]

Corbyn is a radical and a campaigner. The insurgent nature of his leadership campaigns was obvious from the fact that they drew much of their impetus from an activist base built up through this tremendous record of campaigning in mass movements, trade union struggles and solidarity work. The fact that in Britain the new radicalism, uniquely in Europe, is expressing itself within the framework of what has traditionally been a moderate social democratic party, and more recently an extremely right wing one, has led to a massive existential crisis in Labour. The internal struggle is an expression of a growing radicalisation in society colliding with the entrenched elements of the most right-wing Labour parliamentary party ever. Corbyn has faced two leadership challenges, a string of coup attempts and constant low level sabotage. All this will of course have limited his vote. So too will Labour's recent record. Corbyn has fought for a new politics within a party that took Britain into the discredited Afghanistan and Iraq Wars, spent most of the last two and a half decades promoting broadly free market policies and presided over painful cuts in councils up and down the country.

It is important to recognise that this internal battle is far from over. Many of Corbyn's critics and opponents sued for peace more or less graciously after the general election. No doubt there is a reorientation going on, but many in parliament and the party machine hold politics sharply at odds with Corbyn's and those differences are bound to resurface.

The 40 % vote for a programme of renationalisation, redistribution and an end to austerity and further foreign wars was the heaviest blow by far for an already bewildered establishment. It marked a new surge in an already advancing working class consciousness. It is a fantastic basis for a renewed radical politics in Britain and a concerted assault on the neoliberal establishment. But if we are to succeed we need to see it as a platform to rapidly expand and the left not just inside parliament, but on the streets, in the workplaces and our communities.

Understanding Brexit

The Brexit vote too has to be understood in the context of these deep shifts in attitudes. The binary choice of a referendum is always a poor indicator of real opinion. This one was particularly unenlightening, not just because the official debate was so partisan, confused and often racist on both sides, but also because the referendum wasn't asking a question that was on most people's minds. David Cameron called it for party political purposes and it ended up channelling strong feelings into a question most people had previously not been particularly passionate about. Not surprising then that studies of the referendum show that the Leave vote was driven by a complex mix of motives. One thing is clear though: the vote had a strong class element to it. The *Healing a Divided Britain* report found that only the very well off – social group AB – voted in majority to remain in Europe:

> At every level of earning there is a direct correlation between household income and your likelihood to vote for leaving the EU – 62 per cent of those with income of less than £20,000 voted to leave, but that percentage falls in steady increments until, by an income of £60,000, that percentage was just 35 per cent… In short, the people with little or nothing to lose – as they saw it – backed Leave. The ones who had gained most from EU membership and globalisation backed Remain.[31]

Who Voted for Brexit?, the University of Warwick study of voting indicators, found the Leave vote correlated geographically with high growth rates of immigration from Eastern Europe but couldn't identify the exact significance of this correlation. What was clear, however, was that 'areas with strong traditions of manufacturing employment were more likely to vote leave, and also those areas with relatively low pay and high unemployment'. The authors found that austerity policies were also crucial:

> We find that the quality of public service provision is also
> systematically related to the Vote Leave share. In particular,
> fiscal cuts in the context of the recent UK austerity programme
> are strongly associated with a higher Vote Leave share. We
> also produce evidence that lower-quality service provision
> in the National Health Service is associated with the success
> of Vote Leave.

In conclusion they found:

> The voting outcome of the referendum was driven by long-
> standing fundamental determinants, most importantly those
> that make it harder to deal with the challenges of economic
> and social change.[32]

The importance of economic factors is borne out by Lord
Ashcroft's detailed exit poll of voters' social attitudes, notably
the finding that nearly three-quarters (73%) of Remain voters
thought life in Britain is better today than it was 30 years ago;
and a majority (58%) of those who voted to leave say it is
worse. By a majority of 61% to 39% Leave voters also thought
that life would be worse for their children than it had been
for them. Leavers also saw more threats than opportunities to
their standard of living from the way the economy and society
are changing, by 71% to 29% – more than twice the margin
among remainers. Clearly the nature of the vote and the debate
amplified the inclination of some Leavers to see immigration as
the main cause of their problems. But not a majority, according
to Lord Ashcroft's evidence. Just one-third said the main reason
was that leaving 'offered the best chance for the UK to regain
control over immigration and its own borders'. The main reason
cited for voting Leave by the biggest group, just under half, was

'the principle that decisions about the UK should be taken in the UK'.[33] Nor should this response be dismissed as some impulsive protest. It has turned out to be prescient. The progressive programme outlined in Jeremy Corbyn's manifesto would have been much harder to implement had Britain remained at the mercy of the endless EU directives outlawing nationalisation and state intervention.

Concern about immigration was an important factor in the Brexit vote, and it is no secret that racist attitudes endure amongst a significant minority of the British population. This isn't surprising given the level of racism routinely on display in public life. The last 15 years in particular have seen the normalisation of anti-Muslim rhetoric in the media and in political life. Official hostility to immigrants has reached a new intensity in Britain and across Europe as more and more desperate people have fled the carnage and economic chaos created by Western wars and economic policies. It is important, however, to distinguish anxiety about the impact of immigration from hard racist attitudes. The *Healing a Divided Britain* report found that many people's concerns about immigration were not directed at migrants themselves but tended to focus more on 'the impact uncontrolled migration had on wages, access to housing, schools and health care'.[34] But most important of all is to challenge the elite interpretation of the vote as *primarily* anti-immigrant. Such a view is not supported by the evidence and can only suppress the concerns about democracy, economic deprivation and lack of control so clearly expressed in the vote.

Elite dysfunction

Tensions created by Brexit on the left shouldn't obscure the fact that the Brexit vote was a body blow for the British ruling class. British capitalism's big players, the major corporations, the banks and the other financial institutions have long seen membership of the European market as crucial to Britain's future. The post-referendum report from the CBI, Britain's main employers' organisation, lobbied hard for a Brexit that looks pretty much like continued membership.[35] Friction-free trading with Europe is important to a ruling class that has been at the forefront of globalisation. Britain has more foreign direct investment around the world than any other European country. A good deal of this is with Europe. The banks in particular rely on the free flow of European capital in and out of London. But support for EU membership was not just about actual trade with European partners. The closest possible relationship with Europe is regarded as essential for Britain's core economic project of sustaining its role as a financial centre and as a low wage destination for foreign investment from all around the world. Margaret Thatcher was one of the architects and main champions of the European Single Market because it both positioned Britain as a low cost manufacturing base in the European trading area and, through its provisions on the free trade in services, guaranteed against government regulation of the economy. EU membership also helped in the strategic goal of reinforcing the special relationship with the USA. Apart from the immediate economic role as an English-speaking bridgehead for US capital in Europe, successive British governments have pitched themselves to Washington as a reliably neoliberal and hawkish ally in the politically and militarily uncertain European scene, for example, campaigning strongly for the failed free trade agreement between Europe and the Americas.

Despite its paymasters' clear preference, the Tory party itself has long been divided over its attitude to the European Union. Over the years, the Tories have nurtured an ageing, middle class membership suspicious of the Brussels bureaucracy, bigoted about immigration and, in general, jealous about national sovereignty. David Cameron's plan was to promise an EU referendum as a way of undercutting support for UKIP and marginalising the Europhobic right in his own party. Not only did he fail to carry the country, exit polls suggest 58% of Tory voters voted Leave.[36] That the main party of the ruling class is unable to agree on such a key strategic question reveals dysfunction at the heart of the ruling elite and has created massive problems in the short term, let alone further down the line. The Tories are now pursuing a project that is not supported by most of their own leadership or the bulk of the class they represent. The big capitalist interests will be doing everything they can to roll back the decision in practice, while many Tory voters will be pushing for maximum independence and minimum immigration. Every step the Tories take will be fraught with difficulties and the democratic deficit can only grow.

May's gamble of trying of forge a new right wing consensus around a hard Brexit was a disaster. It was always based more on desperation than forward planning and it involved a profound misreading of the public mood. Confounding all the Tories and most pundits' calculations, the general election wasn't mainly about Brexit, immigration or – May's accidental plan B – national security. Economic and social questions dominated partly because the Brexit vote was done and dusted, but also because these were the issues that mainly drove that vote in the first place. Once Team Corby had raised the prospect of state intervention, the rotting shell of Tory politics started to crumble. Planning, redistribution, renationalisation, more democratic participation, all these things are now real possibilities in the minds of millions. In the process the left has regained its rightful ownership of the key question of the day - popular control of society.

The main party of British capitalism is out of sync with its paymasters, its leaders are losing influence over their members and their traditional middle class strongholds let alone the mass of working people, people who regard them with more and more contempt. This at a time when it has no alternative to the programme of austerity that has caused so much of the growing misery and opposition. In the 1930s the Italian Marxist Antonio Gramsci wrote, 'a class is dominant in two ways, that is, it is "leading" and "dominant." It leads the allied classes, and dominates over the adversarial classes'.[37] On both fronts the British ruling class is now failing.

4

The Poverty of Propaganda

Nobody is ever wholly mystified.
Terry Eagleton[1]

The news media has hit a low point. It has never been less diverse in terms of ownership or political approach. Three companies own 71% of national newspaper circulation, Murdoch controls fully a third of this and seven out of the ten top-selling titles backed the Tories in the recent general election with only one backing Labour.[2] Online news is dominated by many of the same organisations that lead in print and TV with the BBC and the Daily Mail out in front.[3] Hand in hand with this concentration has gone a process of commercialisation which has nearly killed off investigative journalism, eroded and intimidated the public service sector and dumbed the media down across the board.

But other things are going on. The growing revolt against neoliberalism is taking place in a situation in which the mainstream media has fully signed up the free market programme. It is universally assumed that state interventionism, let alone socialism, was buried with the twentieth century. As Paul Myerscough explains, this view is important in understanding the BBC and the rest of the liberal media's open contempt for Jeremy Corbyn, expressed in any number of outrageously unbalanced interviews and hostile commentaries:

> Such moments of breakdown in the BBC's editorial principles are a consequence not of the imposition of a producer's or presenter's personal views, but of the dislocation that Corbyn's election has produced between the new state of party politics and the broadcaster's entrenched conception

of what constitutes impartiality. Because its notion of political balance between left and right is defined by the Labour and Conservative Parties, its spectrum of opinion has narrowed and its fulcrum drifted to the right in concert with New Labour. Corbyn has reopened the gap, but the BBC has not adjusted. So far as it is concerned, with his election the Labour leadership has put itself beyond the pale. Its norm remains a 'balance' between the Tories and the Labour right. By defining himself against the establishment, Corbyn becomes an outsider, an insurgent, who can be discussed 'fairly' by the BBC only in the way that, say, Radio 5 Live can 'fairly' cover England's opponents at the World Cup.[4]

This symbiotic relationship between the political and media elites has long worked to limit political discussion. Parliament serves as the reference point for most media comment on politics on the assumption that it accurately reflects public opinion. So for the media, opinion divides into three blocs – a small left, a small right and a big centre. The spectrum tends to be viewed from the middle and outlying opinion on the right and left is termed as 'extreme', 'hard' or 'fringe'. It is regarded as completely static. This is what underlies, for example, BBC *Newsnight* presenter Evan Davis' comment in an interview with Jeremy Corbyn, that, 'only a tiny minority, perhaps one or two million, like your kind of policies', a view now categorically proven as delusional.[5] Not only is it assumed that most people cluster around the centre, but that this 'moderate' middle is the most rational and sensible pace to be. The Middle England model turns out to be a fantasy conjured up out of a swirl of assumptions about geography, class and 'common sense'. It is of course enabled by our distorting electoral system, which most of the time fails drastically to reflect the real mood and opinion of the public. The fact that on most social issues the majority is well to the left of the Westminster media consensus shows that it is more than anything a projection of elite prejudices. Anyone on the left taking it at face value will be drawn to wrong and dangerous conclusions. They will be encouraged to believe that the only way for the left to construct a majority is to 'triangulate'; to assume the loyalty of a left-wing minority, tack to the centre ground to attract the moderate majority and throw in some right-wing policies to win over some reactionaries.

But if this self-serving worship of the centre ground goes some way to explaining media contempt for Corbyn and the left, it is not sufficient. As the left has become more of a threat, the media's attitude has moved beyond prejudice to active and open hostility. Bizarrely, in our version of 'freedom of the press', it is regarded as acceptable for business tycoons to own segments of the media and use them shamelessly to promote their politics. But the lies and vitriol directed against Jeremy Corbyn and his team have recently reached new levels. Personal attacks, lies about the past and fabricated current news stories – fake news frankly - dominated front pages during the June 2017 election. And the open use of news outlets for political ends became normalised across the media spectrum. Research has revealed systematic bias against Corbyn in the liberal bastions of the BBC and the Guardian for example, at least until the Guardian gave Corbyn its last minute and rather reluctant backing.[6] The agenda – even the content – of the right wing press is channelled more and more uncritically by the BBC while it always treated Labour spokespeople much more harshly than those from other parties and routinely recycled Tory attack lines, in one case even reproducing a headline almost word for word from the Conservative website. Its treatment of Corbyn was harsh from the moment he was elected as leader and included ignoring a judgement by its own Trust that it had misrepresented Corbyn and apparently even orchestrating the on-air resignation of an anti-Corbyn shadow cabinet minister.[7]

The bulk of the media was operating on the sinister imperative expressed in the London Evening Standard's editorial on the eve of the election, 'that man cannot be allowed to become Prime Minister'.[8] This is not surprising. The vast majority of media outlets are owned by international media conglomerates. The BBC is run by a board mainly appointed by the government. Its executives are paid £300,000 plus, went to elite universities and have often worked for the right wing press. Head of News James Harding worked for the Financial Times and the Times before the BBC. Sarah Sands, the new editor of the flagship Today Programme, was the editor of the Evening Standard and the Sunday Telegraph and has also worked for the Daily Mail and the Telegraph.

The more and more hysterical bias of the media is a product of the fact that its growing integration into the corporate world has coincided with a more and more organised popular opposition. The twist is, however, that as this happens the bias becomes more obvious. A poll taken during Corbyn's second election campaign in 2016 found that 51% of the population thought the media was deliberately biased against Corbyn and only 29% didn't.[9] Just as other elite institutions have suffered legitimacy problems, an openly establishment media can quickly lose its ability to shape ideas. This has opened the way for the widespread and effective use of movement based social media that has made a huge contribution in promoting Corbyn's radical policies and popularising alternatives to the mainstream. It has profound implications. Such potential limits to the elites' persuasive powers need to be factored into how we think about the way people's ideas are shaped in capitalist society.

Propaganda's limits

The left has important critical approaches to draw on. In the USA, Noam Chomsky and his collaborators have developed an influential account of why the media is biased called 'the propaganda model'. The virtue of this approach is its attempt to explain media behaviour by placing it within a context of powerful interests. Its starting point is that 'the media serve the interests of state and corporate power, which are closely interlinked, framing their reporting and their analysis in a manner supportive of established privilege and limiting discussion and debate accordingly'.[10] It identifies five 'filters' which ensure that media output generally reflects or supports the interests of the elites. One of those involves direct outside pressure: 'government and large non-media business firms are also best positioned (and sufficiently wealthy) to be able to pressure the media with threats of withdrawal of advertising or TV licences, libel suits and other direct and indirect modes of attack'.[11] But it is not a theory based only on direct, conscious intervention:

> The crucial structural factors derive from the fact that the dominant media are embedded in the market system. They are profit making businesses, owned by very wealthy people; they are funded largely by advertisers who are also profit making entities, and who want their ads to appear in a supportive selling environment. The media are also dependent on government and major business firms as information sources, and both efficiency and political considerations, and frequently overlapping interests, cause a certain degree of solidarity to prevail among the government, major media, and other corporate businesses.[12]

The propaganda model provides a suggestive account of the reinforcing ways in which ruling elites influence media messaging. It is a much needed antidote to the static approach of the mainstream. But, for all its critical insight, in Chomsky's model, the traffic is all one way. Leaving aside the assumption that people actually believe what the media says, the model fails to explore the contradictions in the media or allow for any feedback from popular opinion. It can leave you with the impression that the media has almost hypnotic powers. In this sense, it is part of a wider tendency on the left. Ruling classes instinctively tend to believe in the universal appeal of their worldview, but some on the left have also long been over-impressed by the elite's persuasive powers and in awe of their 'soft power'. Perry Anderson has noted Marxist intellectuals' tendency to focus on the 'study of superstructures' since the ebbing of the revolutionary wave of the 1920s. This involved a move away from economic and political problems. It was both a product and a cause of pessimism.[13]

From the Frankfurt School to Foucault and beyond, left theorists have developed a series of strong models of ideological power. The experience of fascism and post war capitalist stabilisation led some on the left to despair of the possibility of mass radicalisation. In the boom years Adorno and Horkheimer's *The Dialectic of the Enlightenment* and Herbert Marcuse's *One-Dimensional Man* both influentially argued that the capitalist world was effectively closed to challenge.[14]

Denying the real

Similar ideas spread further still after the defeat of the great radical wave of the 1960s and 1970s. French philosopher and historian Michel Foucault provided perhaps the most influential account of all-pervading power in capitalist society. He argued that power is inscribed into everything we do: 'the proletariat has been thoroughly imbued with bourgeois ideology concerning morality and legality, concerning theft and crime'.[15] Links between class and ideology and between state and power couldn't explain this situation: 'power is not something that is acquired, seized or shared, something that one holds on to or allows to slip away; power is exercised from innumerable points'.[16] As Aijaz Ahmad has pointed out, for all Foucault's brilliance as a historian and archivist, his guiding concept of 'a power which permeates everything and reproduces itself copiously in all the pores of society' ruled out the existence of a reality free from power relations and ultimately made a challenge to it near impossible. Even the existence of an independent reality was brought into question.[17]

Some of Foucault's successors went on to invest language with the power to construct meaning independently of humans, completing, in the words of a critic, Christopher Norris, 'a retreat from any theory capable of mustering resistance to received ideologies'.[18] Postmodernism completely abandoned the project of understanding society in its totality. The tendency reached its notorious low point in the 1990s when post-modernist guru Jean Baudrillard published a book called *The Gulf War Did Not Take Place,* in which he argued that the first Gulf War was an elaborate fraud and not really a war at all.[19]

These kind of extreme positions have been widely challenged. But scepticism about grand narratives and humans' ability to understand the world has real penetration. It has been a godsend for the ruling class in their attempts to convince us 'there is no alternative', and doubts about our ability to see beyond immediate reality have infected the left. We have seen how the British theorists of 'new times' talked up the power of encroaching commodification to shape people's sense of reality in the 1980s. There are echoes of this in recent explanations of the system's staying power. In *Capitalist Realism,* for example, Mark Fisher argued that 'for most people under twenty in Europe and North America, the lack of alternatives to capitalism is no longer even an issue. Capitalism seamlessly occupies the horizons of the thinkable'.[20]

The propaganda model also remains highly influential. *Flat Earth News*, Nick Davies' seminal account of the degrading of the British media in the era of neoliberalism, ends with a despairing quote from one of its advocates, Robert McChesney:

The type of political culture that accompanies the rise of the corporate media system worldwide looks to be increasingly like that found in the United States: in the place of informed debate or political parties organizing along the full spectrum of opinion, there will be vacuous journalism and elections dominated by public relations, big money, moronic political advertising, and limited debate on tangible issues. It is a world where the market and commercial values overwhelm notions of democracy and civic culture, a world where depoliticization runs rampant , and a world where the wealthy few face fewer and fewer threats of political challenge.[21]

Such analyses contain important insights and describe real mechanisms of intellectual and social control. But they dramatically overstate their case. In their focus on the 'soft power' of modern capitalism, they underplay the many elements of capitalist experience that tend towards rebellion and resistance.

The education of experience
This is why it is important to reassert Marx's core insight – developed by a string of successors, including notably Antonio Gramsci, Georg Lukács and Rosa Luxemburg – that consciousness is a product more than anything of *contradictory experience*. In this view ideas can change dramatically in the heat of crisis and social struggle. This approach provides a crucial corrective to the mainstream's static, sociological mapping of popular opinion and to the closed loop of power proposed by Foucault and his followers. It provides some important context too to the many insights of Chomsky's model of propaganda power. By seeing ideas as the product of the experience of a divided society, Marxism helps explain both capitalism's ability to win acceptance most of the time and its tendency to generate

resistance at others. Like Chomsky, Marx was always clear that the ruling class is at pains to disseminate its own view of the world through the institutions of capitalist society:

> The ideas of the ruling class are in every epoch the ruling ideas, i.e. the class which is the ruling material force of society, is at the same time its ruling intellectual force. The class which has the means of material production at its disposal, has control at the same time over the means of mental production, so that thereby, generally speaking, the ideas of those who lack the means of mental production are subject to it.[22]

But for Marx the institutions of propaganda and persuasion in capitalist society are only one aspect of the way in which bourgeois ideas dominate. He was the first to grasp the way commodification helped to conceal the systematic robbery at the heart of capitalism:

> The finished pattern of economic relations as seen on the surface in their real existence... is very different and indeed quite the reverse of and antagonistic to their inner, essential, but concealed core and the concepts corresponding to it.[23]

This is the result of what Marx called alienation. The very nature of the way profit is extracted from the worker creates a sense of powerlessness. The worker is treated like a cog in a machine. In the words of Hungarian Marxist Georg Lukács, the result is, 'the personality can do no more than look on hopelessly while its own existence is reduced to an isolated particle and fed into an alien system'.[24]

Such alienated labour produces 'commodities', goods whose primary purpose is to be bought and sold. Commodity production dominates society to such an extent that it appears to reduce life to a series of exchanges between things. Workers themselves effectively become commodities on the labour market. Commodity logic shapes our very personalities: 'It stamps its imprint upon the whole consciousness of man; his qualities and abilities are no longer an organic part of his personality, they are things he can "own" or "dispose of" like the various objects of the outside world'.[25]

Capitalist ideology consists of a series of formal universal laws and systems of thought that both reflect and reinforce this atomised, commodified reality. But this is just one side of the story. For Marx and subsequent revolutionaries these universal laws fail, in fact, to incorporate effectively other important aspects of lived experience. In particular, they cannot contain an explosive contradiction at the heart of the way capitalism functions. There is a problem with commodifying humans' labour power. Unlike all other commodities, labour power is a commodity connected to a brain. Franz Jakubowski explains this in one of the best Marxist accounts of capitalist ideology, written in the 1930s:

Because the proletarian experiences this relationship both as object and subject, he is in a position to see through the fetish appearance of the commodity labour power. The worker can see that value is not an organic, inherent attribute of the commodity labour power, for he knows that this commodity is at the same time man, a legal subject, who, outside production, is judged not by his material value, but as the equal of other men.[26]

In practice, the necessity for the capitalist to drive down workers' wages and attack conditions means that the commodification of labour always risks a pushback. What appears to the capitalist as a mere quantitative reduction in wages or lengthening of the working day can be for the worker a qualitative break, a life-changing, sometimes even life-threatening event. This doesn't mean that workers automatically see beyond the commodity relation, but it does mean that the possibility is always there. Once workers become aware of the way in which their human capacities are quantified and used in capitalist production, then the real relations of capitalist production can start to become clear. Again in Lukács' words, in some circumstances at least, 'this transformation of a human function into a commodity reveals in all its starkness the dehumanised and dehumanising function of the commodity relation'.[27]

Working-class experience then, turns out to be the key source of radical consciousness. Capitalism creates misery and resistance amongst many groups outside the working class, and special grievances amongst many subsets of working people. But workers have a unique potential to both grasp the need for radical change and to mount an effective challenge to the system. Even in boom times when capitalism is generating enough profits to concede some improvement in living standards, class experience is decisive. Capitalists are still looking to raise profits by reducing wages. The very decision to join and get active in a union is a recognition of a fundamental antagonism in society and an expression of a basic class consciousness.

As attacks on working people have intensified and generalised into an assault on a wide range of social democratic gains, it is no wonder that there has been a growing sense of class resentment. Not only have we seen a massive shift in income from working people to the rich, the commercialisation of new areas of life has also been associated with a dramatic decline in security, stability and well-being. When the crash revealed the fictitious nature of much of the debt that was being sold, it was a sign both of the chaotic nature of the economic system and the dishonesty of those running it. Crisis has stripped away the credibility of the market; it has thrown into question the elite's basic ability to organise society. It has also begun to reveal the active elements of class rule and the relationships between different parts of the state that are normally concealed by the apparently automatic or impersonal functioning of the market. In these circumstances, the collaboration between sections of the state can become a liability for the system. In particular, media support for the status quo can reveal its bias and undermine its propaganda value.

Not that economic crises automatically reveal capitalist relations in full. Crises play out in complex ways and spread out over space and time. But the tendency is toward multiple revelations:

> The further the economic crisis of capitalism advances, the more this unity in the economic process becomes comprehensible in practice... For even if the particular symptoms of crisis appear separate (according to the country, branch of industry, in the form of 'economic' or 'political' crisis etc.), and even if in consequence the reflex of the crisis is fragmented in the immediate psychological consciousness of the workers, it is still possible and still necessary to advance beyond this consciousness. And this is instinctively felt by larger and larger sections of the proletariat.[28]

In the beginning was the deed

Everyday experience, then, ensures that working people tend to have an instinctive suspicion of big business, big bosses and the free market. This is the reason for the stubbornness of social democratic and collective ideas amongst workers even in difficult times. The combination of class aggression and crisis we are currently experiencing was bound to sharpen these attitudes. Now this critical consciousness has started to take organised expression, and as we shall see in the final chapter, the question of exactly how it organises itself will be a matter of vital significance as the crisis unfolds. But it is important to note in the meantime that nothing spreads clarity and understanding about capitalist class relations more effectively than mass struggle, the active embodiment of human being's ability to co-operate to change things. Participatory struggles are important because they can lead to victories, but also because they are profoundly educational. On the occasions when workers start to fight back collectively, their essential, strategic role in the capitalist system is confirmed and their interests in unity and solidarity – in overcoming division and commodification – are underlined. When workers' resistance starts to take off, its potential to bring the system to a halt can become clear. The logic of supply and demand, of the freedom to labour and the rights to property are suddenly revealed to be superficial, no longer successfully concealing the deeper class relations that underpin them.

It is in the process of great strikes and campaigns, protests and riots that people begin to understand quickest their own power and to work out who are their friends and who their enemies. When struggles generalise, the courts, the police the media are forced to take sides openly and in the process the real landscape of class power can be revealed. Faced with real and coherent opposition the ruling class has to either make concessions or take repressive measures. This either legitimates the opposition or exposes the elite's contempt for democracy. Polish revolutionary Rosa Luxemburg insisted on the educational and cultural value of mass struggles:

The most precious, lasting, thing in the rapid ebb and flow of the wave is its mental sediment: the intellectual, cultural growth of the proletariat, which proceeds by fits and starts, and which offers an inviolable guarantee of their further irresistible progress in the economic as in the political struggle.[29]

Genuinely mass struggles, especially when they are centred on workplace organisation, help provide evidence of the power of collective struggle, begin to overcome the atomisation of capitalist society and start to crystallise communities of interests that are latent in capitalism. To those involved, they start to suggest the possibility of a way out of alienation. Great national or international struggles have an impact even beyond those who are involved, shaping politics and profoundly influencing the way large numbers of people understand the world. For Marx, this property of struggle was one of the main reasons why revolutionary activity is so important:

Both for the production on a mass scale of this communist consciousness, and for the success of the cause itself, the alteration of men on a mass scale is necessary, an alteration which can only take place in a practical movement, a revolution; this revolution is necessary, therefore, not only because the ruling class cannot be overthrown in any other way, but also because the class overthrowing it can only in a revolution succeed in ridding itself of all the muck of ages and become fitted to found society anew.30

5

Where Are the Workers?

We are all middle class now.
John Prescott[1]

It is ironic that in an era when such huge resources have been deployed to attack the working class, there has been such a concerted effort to deny its existence. We have seen how arch class warrior Margaret Thatcher tried to intellectually dissolve not just class but society itself into the categories of individual and family. Slightly less ambitiously, her successor John Major announced in 1990 that he wanted a 'classless society'. Labour wasn't far behind. Tony Blair's advisor Andrew Adonis agreed that rising living standards meant 'the old labels of "working class" and "middle class" make less and less sense'.[2]

No one nowadays bothers much to challenge the idea of a ruling class. The concentration of wealth and power in the hands of the owners of big capital is so blatant that it can't be completely denied. But the existence of a working class is still a matter of controversy. Sociologists love to fragment the working population in their modelling. The widely reported *Great British Class Survey* carried out in 2013 by academics Mike Savage and Fiona Devine, for example, found that the 'traditional working class' was just one of seven classes in today's society including 'the precariat' and 'new affluent workers'. This breakup of traditional class categories was prefigured in the Blair government's view that society was divided into various grades of hard working consumers on the one hand and the feckless unemployed on the other. The political focus was on what it called 'the underclass', poor and largely workless people, mainly living on estates, whose attitudes needed to be changed and whose anti-social tendencies needed to be monitored and where necessary punished. A social exclusion unit was set up in 1998 to do precisely that, with disastrous results.[3]

There are more radical versions of similar ideas. Guy Standing's foregrounding of the precariat in modern capitalism is among the most influential. He argues precarious workers are crucial to the new neoliberal global economy, which has replaced the relatively stable factory-driven regime of accumulation. The result is the rapid decline of anything resembling the old proletariat and the emergence of a precarious class with its own interests:

> The precariat is in the front ranks, but it has yet to find the voice to bring its agenda to the fore. It is not the 'squeezed middle' or an 'underclass' or 'the lower working class'. It has a distinctive bundle of insecurities and will have an equally distinctive set of demands.[4]

Another trend is to downgrade the importance of work in defining class. Amazingly, the *Great British Class Survey* doesn't even regard occupation as worthy of recording in its 'calculator' of modern class categories. Its questionnaire asks only about income, housing, savings, the kind of people you know and what you do in your leisure time.[5] This downplaying of work is part of a tendency to see identity as something defined by consumption and lifestyle. Pierre Bourdieu provided a specific theoretical tool to facilitate this approach when he proposed 'cultural capital' as one of three or four forms that capital could take in modern society.[6] Other types of identity politics, which regard gender, sexual orientation and race as our most important defining characteristics, have also contributed to 'a retreat from class', even on the left.[7]

More recent writers have suggested that work is becoming marginal for capitalism itself. In *PostCapitalism*, Paul Mason argues that new technologies are creating networks of people who are effectively communicating and exchanging outside the logic and control of capitalist markets, thus creating the possibility of moving beyond it. So 'work, the defining activity of capitalism, is losing its centrality both to exploitation and resistance'.[8] In a rather darker register Srnicek and Williams argue in *Inventing the Future* that wage labour is declining in economic importance, creating both increased precarity, and 'surplus populations' whose lives are controlled in more and more authoritarian ways.[9]

What these different positions share is the sense that the political project based around the working class is over. As Bryan Palmer argues, the level of structural change in Guy Standing's model of precariat capitalism implies that:

> stable working-class identities have been swept aside; a sense of proletarian power as a transformative agent of social relations of exploitation and oppression is now ended.[10]

I do mind dying

Working life has indeed been transformed by the last 40 years of neoliberal shock and awe. Defined in terms of collective workplace organisation and strike days lost, class struggle in Britain is at a low ebb. Strikes are still rare and although there has been a slight pickup in the last five years, union organisation is alarmingly weak, particularly in the private sector, where only 14% of employees are in a union.[11] The defeats of organised labour and the rundown of highly unionised industries over the last 40 years have taken a heavy toll. The nature of work and the makeup of the workforce, have also changed dramatically. Manufacturing industry now accounts for just 10% of jobs and roughly the same percentage of the gross domestic product.[12] There has been a huge increase in jobs in communication, finance, marketing, tourism, retail and services generally.

There are fewer permanent and full time jobs than there were 30 years ago, and a massive increase in the number of women in the workforce has broken the 'traditional' pattern of men as the main breadwinners. The workforce also reflects a society that has become much more ethnically mixed over the last decades, a trend that has increased recently as employers have actively sought cheap workers from abroad, most recently from Eastern Europe.

But the idea that we are moving into a post-work society or that the working class is no longer a useful category is hard to square with two basic facts. First, the workforce is bigger than ever before, with over 30 million working, more than 75% of the population, the highest percentage since 1971.[13] Second, as we have seen, society is more and more economically polarised, with the vast majority suffering real terms income loss while a tiny minority has grown progressively wealthier. If class is conceived in terms of particular industries or technologies, or in terms of particular types of working practices or contractual relationships, it will always appear fragmented or indeed vanishing, such is the speed of change in capitalist economies. Rapid technological and economic change has always impacted dramatically and unevenly on working lives. As late as the 1890s, at the time Britain was proverbially known as the workshop of the world, agriculture employed more than any single industrial group. Industry was concentrated in specific regions mainly outside of the capital, while London was dominated by service industries – including the docks – which often employed high levels of casual labour.[14]

The kind of industry that a person works in is not what defines their class position. In our highly commodified society, almost all production and the majority of what are defined as services are produced directly for profit. What is decisive is an individual's relationship to that process of profit making. The labour power of a catering worker, a cleaner, a receptionist, a train driver, a bankworker or a phone salesperson is expended in the pursuit of corporate profit, and regulated and controlled by corporate managements. This is what makes all of these people working class. Even the shrinking public sector is organised to complement private industry by fulfilling necessary functions that big business hasn't yet managed to exploit. More and more public sector organisations have been turned into administrative shells, desperately trying to limit the damage and chaos of enforced outsourcing. The result is more and more public servants have ended up working for profiteering companies, degrading services and working conditions.

Attitudes to particular types of work change over time. The spread of Fordist factory production in the first part of the twentieth century is now associated with the high points of working-class organisation. But when the first car plants opened in Britain in the 1930s they were dismissed as unorganisable. Car workers were regarded as a highly paid highly skilled elite inherently hostile to trade unionism. The service sector has always been important in the British working class – until at least the 1920s domestic servants constituted the largest single group in the workforce, and manufacturing workers have never been an overall majority.[15] But until the 1960s, most of the service sector was regarded as of secondary importance for the unions. As the service sector has expanded, jobs in retail, catering, hospitals, financial services and local government have become progressively more routine and regimented. The supermarket, the warehouse and the call centre are pace setters in automation and division of labour. Though it is difficult to source figures on UK workplace size, many of them are large workplaces too. Tesco, for example, one of the biggest private sector employers in the UK, has concentrated its distribution into half a dozen massive warehouses across the country. Figures for the USA suggest that workplace size has remained stable over the last 35 years, with 45% working in workplaces of over 100 employees in

2007 as opposed to 46% in 1980.[16] Various sectors of the service industry, including postal services and retail, have now become important centres of trade unionism.

Nor is casualisation anything new. Employers have always encouraged precarious conditions where possible. The radical tradition has long recognised that the unemployed, casualised and underemployed play an important role in the labour market, taking up the slack in boom times and helping to 'discipline' the wider workforce the rest of the time. Marx wrote in *Capital*:

> The lowest sediment of the relative surplus-population finally dwells in the sphere of pauperism... the quantity of paupers increases with every crisis... Pauperism is the hospital of the active labour-army and the dead weight of the industrial reserve army. Its production is included in that of the relative surplus population, its necessity in theirs; along with the surplus population, pauperism forms a condition of capitalist production, and of the capitalist development of wealth.[17]

Recent experience bears out the idea that the unemployed or casualised are not, in fact, separate from the wider workforce. An academic study in the 1990s following the lives of working people in Britain put the lie to the government notion of a permanent underclass. It concluded that many working people found themselves in serious poverty at various times in their lives due to unemployment or low wages: 'many more people are "touched" by poverty and receive short-term help from the benefit system than might at first appear'.[18] Studies of contemporary trends suggest that still only a small minority of workers are on short-term contracts, and that most people who enter the labour market on those terms find more secure work as they get older, although the gender differential is stark. While 16% of 18 to 21-year-olds are on temporary contracts, by the age of 25 that figure goes down to 7%. The figures for part-time work are higher, and much higher for women. 33% of women work less than 30 hours a week in their thirties.[19] But this fact reflects the appalling level of childcare support in Britain rather than actual precarity. Combining all non-full time and non-permanent contracts in one precarious category obscures rather than clarifies the situation. These are real changes going on that require a serious strategic response from the left and the labour movement. But permanent and full-time jobs remain the majority experience, and the facts don't support the idea of a new, separate precarious class.

Becoming conscious

Class has both an objective as well as a subjective dimension. Workers play a particular and indispensable role in capitalist society whether they are aware of it or not; they produce the goods and services that are essential to keeping society running and to the production of profits for the owners of business. The idea that workers are becoming less strategically important is impossible to sustain. For all British capitalism's chronic problems, the amount of wealth being produced in society is greater than ever before, and the surplus continues to be largely siphoned off by the big corporations. Without workers, the tiny minority who own significant amounts of wealth would be unable to expand its value, something they have to do to stay competitive.

This doesn't mean that workers always understand their own role or position. Marx made the important distinction between the 'class in itself' and the class fully aware of its interests and therefore 'for itself'. Theories that downplay the objective role of workers in the process of production tend to be intensely ideological. Their focus on consumption and lifestyle obscures rather than illuminates people's social position. As consumers, we are encouraged to feel equal even if our spending power is wildly uneven. If we have some extra cash, we may try and express ourselves as best we can through the purchase of various commodities. But such limited choice doesn't cancel inequality, cannot really define us as human beings nor restore any control over our working lives.

If neoliberalism has broken up some of the traditional bastions of working-class collectivity and relentlessly promoted the individual as the beginning and end of wisdom, it has also extended corporate control over new areas of life and increased the number of people in the service of big capital. Given the experience of the last few decades it is perhaps no wonder then that all polls show that a growing number of people – 60% and upwards – see themselves as working-class.[20] Even most people who regard themselves as middle-class think that the crucial division is between the richest 1% and the rest. Selina Todd summarises her fascinating account of working lives over the last hundred years by emphasising continuity. She argues that today's workforce shares many attitudes with that of 30 or 50 years ago. Of her recent study she says, 'those people who considered themselves working-class did so primarily for the same reason given by earlier generations: they had to work for a living'.[21]

Militants and movements

If a sense of class is making a comeback, what about class struggle? The truth is class combativity and cohesion have never been automatic and always had to be argued and campaigned for. Divisions, defeat, disorientating economic change and ruling-class propaganda can all make resistance seem difficult. But these are obstacles that have repeatedly been overcome in the forging of class-based resistance. The birth of mass unionism in the late 1880s was partly the product of tireless work by a talented generation of socialists trained in the first socialist parties in Britain. The great 'unorganisable' new industries which sprung up in suburban areas in the Midlands and the South East in the 1930s and 1940s were often organised by socialist veterans who had migrated from the slump-hit mining and dock industries of the North, Scotland and South Wales.[22] The extension of working class organisation of the early 1970s was boosted by the great international radicalisation after 1968. Helped by the general politicisation and the tremendous example of militant action in the mines, docks, car plants and across manufacturing, a new generation of activists established strong union organisation and class identification in previously weak sectors of education, public services, the post offices and so on.

Trade union organisation and struggle is stuck at very low levels. And the left needs to turn its attention to overcoming this weakness because organised workplace based resistance is the necessary centrepiece of any successful struggle for social transformation. But a sense of perspective is important. With more than 6 million members, the trade unions remain by far the biggest organisations of any kind in British society and they bring together workers of all backgrounds. Women are more likely to be trade unionists than men and there is a higher density of trade unionists amongst Afro-Caribbean workers than amongst white workers. The unions are held together by networks of tens of thousands of activists and shop stewards and the trade unions regularly organise impressive protests and demonstrations and national and sometimes local strikes have a big impact on society.[23]

Nor should we try to read off the future from the past in a mechanical way. The dramatic changes of the last few decades present us with new strategic and theoretical challenges. The scale of the offensive on working people has had a complex effect on consciousness. On the one hand, it has made a repeat of the exact pattern of radicalisation last time around seem unlikely. During the 1950s and 1960s, working-class strength was accumulated over time largely by a series of sectional strikes, often organised on a local basis, independently of the national organisation of the unions. In boom conditions it made sense for employers to settle disputes relatively quickly to keep profitable production running. This 'do it yourself reformism' generated impressive levels of trade union density and a rank and file militancy that reached its high point in the great struggles against the Tories in the early 1970s. This is a history that probably won't be re-enacted exactly.

On the other hand, the scale and breadth of the attacks on working people and the class hostility on display from the full spectrum of capitalist institutions has generated a wider politicisation. All this, combined with Labour's buy-in to big business in the Blair years, helped generate a different, more political kind of self-activity. Early last decade, labour expert John Godard noticed a new generalisation amongst British workers:

In current economic times, there is no doubt a widespread and growing sense of injustice, but this appears to be directed more at the political and economic system in general, especially in Britain. So while the institutionalization of conflict thesis popular in the post-war era essentially argued that the genius of the post-war system was its ability to contain the manifestation of broader labor-capital conflicts by institutionalizing and addressing them within the employment relation, it might now be possible to speak of the 'deinstitutionalization' of conflict and its manifestation outside of the economic sphere, in the form of political or social instability.[24]

Godard's view is borne out by a large but largely unreported growth in popular protest in Britain and many other countries.

Both the *World Values Survey* and the *British Social Attitudes Survey* showed a remarkable increase in political protesting between the 1970s and 1980s and last decade. Whereas in 1983 only 2% of the British population admitted going on an anti-government demonstration, this percentage had risen to 10% by 2006.[25] More recent research suggests that the level of protest has increased since then, and that 2015 was a highpoint. One study found that '2015 actually had the highest level of visible dissent in the UK since before the 1980s'.[26] Harvard political scientist Pippa Norris has been tracking and analysing this trend over the last few decades. She argues that 'the political energies among the younger generation in post-industrial societies have diversified and flowed through cause-oriented activism, rather than simply ebbed away into apathy'.[27] She goes on to connect this with the impact of neoliberalism on the political realm:

> The 'shrinkage of the state' through initiatives such as privatization, marketization, and deregulation means that decision making has flowed away from public bodies and official government agencies that were directly accountable to elected representatives... reinforcing the need for alternative avenues and targets of political expression and mobilization.[28]

In the last two decades in particular there have been cycles of mass popular action in many different parts of the world that have articulated growing anger and alienation at the neoliberal order and often brought organised workers and the traditional left together with wider constituencies. The Chiapas uprising led by the Zapatista movement in Mexico in 1994 and the combined strike wave and social movement in France in 1995 were the first real challenges to elite complacency after the fall of the Berlin Wall. Mass anti-capitalism hit popular consciousness with the extraordinary protests against the WTO in Seattle in December

1999 that brought together trade unionists and environmentalists – 'teamsters and turtles' – in a series of confrontations with the police that hit TV screens around the world. Seattle was a turning point. The WTO was disrupted and the creative heroics on display from this new coalition in the heart of the beast and the home of Microsoft galvanised organising globally.

In the years that followed, anti-capitalist protest and convergence drew millions of people into activism, and the global elites were forced to stop meeting in urban centres like Seattle, Nice, Genoa and Washington by huge protests. They retreated to mountain refuges and remote islands. A wave of popular radicalisation in Latin America shook whole regimes and removed governments as the decade went on. The protesting and networking helped lay the groundwork for the historic popular response to Bush and Blair's war on Iraq in 2003 which generated the biggest protest in world history and years of creative mass anti-war campaigning in many parts of the world. By the time of the banking crisis in 2008, a precedent of mass street and community protest had been established, which carried over into the post-crash world. In many places working-class organisation played a central role. In Greece, street mobilisations combined with a cycle of general strikes to force a political crisis that ultimately led to the election of the Syriza government. Economic anger helped fuel the 2011 uprisings in Tunisia and Egypt, in the process sparking a new wave of factory struggles.

In Britain the anti-austerity movement took some time to gather after the banking crisis. But the anti-war movement had created a model and the inspiration of the Occupy movement, UK Uncut actions, protests by disability activists, huge trade union demonstrations and important one-day strikes helped to cohere the sense of common action and generate enthusiasm for an anti-austerity coalition. The People's Assembly was launched at a 4,000-strong conference in the summer of 2012 and helped organise the movement and connect it to a wider constituency. As Alex Nunns, one of the chroniclers of Corbyn's rise, has explained, the People's Assembly and the wider movements were crucial to the campaign:

> It was the movement that brought the magic to the Corbyn campaign. Although a process was already underway within the Labour membership, seen in the CLP nominations and early canvassing returns, what gave the Corbyn phenomenon its particular character was the participation of people from outside the party. It was the sense that Jeremy Corbyn was at the head of a broad movement that made his leadership bid so extraordinary. The excitement; the dynamism; the heady disorientating feeling of the impossible becoming possible – these were the trappings of movement politics.[29]

In its own way, then, Britain was conforming to a wider pattern. Mass social movements were expressing the anger that people felt but were unable to register through normal channels. These movements were mobilising workers in the streets who mostly didn't yet have the confidence or the organisation to mount resistance at work. In the process they radicalised those who participated and many who didn't, and now they have impacted on politics. The crucial question now is can these developments lead to a return to working-class confidence and combativity itself? There are some signs that this can happen. By making issues out of privatisation and austerity, low pay and inequality, protest campaigns have helped to create the conditions that can encourage workers to escalate to industrial action. In the last few years, creative strategies adopted by the NUT have seen teachers and teaching assistants organising high profile strikes and campaigns that have deliberately used social movement tactics to build momentum and support. They have called mass demonstrations and community protests, participated in wider mobilisations and actively campaigned for solidarity on a political basis in the wider working class. Junior doctors, tube workers and rail workers too have recently staged effective action that has connected with people's concerns about the future of the NHS and transport safety. Various union campaigns have started to focus on the lowest paid and the precarious. Unite the union has exposed and shamed nineteenth-century working conditions in Sports Direct warehouses, causing a crisis in the company. Casualised delivery workers at Deliveroo have staged protests and walkouts against changes to their contracts. These modest initiatives are not going to make a dent in the strike statistics, but they suggest possibilities. While industrial action remains at low levels there are signs of a rise in the number of ballots taking place, in turnout and in the size of votes for action. In a situation in which general opposition to government policy is growing, strategic strike action can attract popular support and take resistance to new levels. Polling showed that, despite anti-strike hysteria in the media, the junior doctors had overwhelming public support for their campaign.[30] For decades now working class political consciousness has outstripped workplace-based combativity. The eruption of support for Corbyn is the latest, most dramatic expression of this. This imbalance needs to be overcome, but it is at the intersection of politics and economics that class combativity is most likely to re-emerge. We must use the enthusiasm and the radicalisation generated by the Corbynism to reinvigorate workplace organisation and struggle as a matter of urgency.

6

Socialists and System Failure

*We live in capitalism, its power seems inescapable. So did the
divine right of kings.*
Ursula Le Guin[1]

The establishment's problems run deep. The neoliberal assault
involved an attempt to break up the post-war settlement.
Though it succeeded in transferring enormous levels of wealth
from poor to rich, it has run up against two great problems.
First, though it was presented as an attempt to deal with low
levels of growth, profitability and investment, neoliberalism
has done nothing to solve these underlying economic problems.
All three basic metrics remain at unimpressive levels. Even the
relatively modest growth achieved in the last couple of decades
has been fuelled by unsustainable levels of debt. The situation is
now worse than it was before the banking crisis; debt has grown
again, surging on the back of government bailouts and cheap
money, and there is intense nervousness about the weakness of
the economy and fact that central banks don't have the reserves
to deal with further shocks. More fundamentally, there is good
evidence that high debt, rising inequality and low growth are
having a mutually reinforcing effect.[2] But despite these long-
term trends and the devastating impact of the banking crash,
there has been no change of economic course since 2008. The
real significance of the paralysis in the Tory Party and turmoil
in the ruling class is that their economic project is unsustainable,
but they have developed no alternative. What we are seeing is
not just the faltering of neoliberalism, but the unfolding of a
profound crisis of the capitalist system.

Secondly the ruling class has run up against the fact that

most 'ordinary' people prefer the idea of a society based on some social solidarity to one driven solely by the vagaries of the free market and the interests of the super-rich. As long as working people were persuaded – by defeat, demoralisation and poor leadership – that such ideas were incompatible with the modern world, the neoliberals could sustain their scam. But the obvious failure of the economic model helped unlock accumulated resentment, deepened a sense of class, undermined the authority of elite ideas and institutions opened up space for the promotion of alternatives. The anti-capitalist movement that mobilised hundreds of thousands at the start of the twenty-first century helped popularise a critique of globalised capitalism but was unable to break out of its activist base, impressive though that was. The Iraq War, and later the banking crisis and state support for the resulting corporate and financial assault, all radicalised society much further. Protest movements were strengthened, re-invigorating existing activists and beginning to influence and involve new sections of the public, including young people, ultimately lending energy and impetus to Corbyn's leadership bid. Once mass opinion, mass movements, and a mass political project started to assert alternatives the core project of the ruling class was thrown into doubt.

This, then, is an explosive situation in which, to paraphrase Lenin, the ruling class cannot continue in the old way, and the working class doesn't want to. There are three registers that are important in making the most of it. First, there is the opportunity that Corbyn's rise presents. Corbyn has invigorated the left, made socialism a discussion point, given expression to a pent up demand for radical change and turned a general ruling class malaise into a sharp political crisis. Any serious strategy for change involves backing the Corbyn project to the hilt. But we also need to be realistic about its limits and vulnerabilities, including the dangers posed by the Labour right in parliament. This leads to the second set of considerations.

The left needs to develop ways to push the project forward and keep pushing the right back, but, particularly given Corbyn's trials and tribulations, it is vital that the movement's horizons are not limited to parliament. The continued development of mass participatory movements is essential if we are to make any headway. Recent international experience shows that the wholesale transfer of aspirations for change from the street, workplaces and communities to parliament is a dangerous mistake. While what happens in parliament is critically important, society's basic direction of travel will mainly be decided elsewhere and, paradoxically, the stronger the left becomes in parliament, the *more* outside pressure is needed, as opposition from the right and state bodies will grow. Most commentators ignore the importance of the social movements, but as this short history has shown, a series of great social struggles have decisively shaped British life in the last few decades. The final question concerns specifically socialist organisation. Another apparent paradox is that independent, socialist organisation is an essential element of building broad movements of resistance. To elaborate a thoroughgoing critique of the crisis, to develop a joined up strategy for change, and to try and popularise them both, those who are committed to fundamental change from below need to be working and organising together.

Labour and the crisis

The immediate reason for the Tories' poor performance in the June 2017 election was that they were faced with a left wing Labour leadership that went on to the attack for the first time in a generation. It is true the the Tories stumbled into the election with many problems. They were split over Brexit, economic direction, social attitudes and more. May's leadership was weak, and the manifesto shambolic. But most of the media and her own party were happy to back her and would have cheered her all the way to Downing Street. The plan was in fact that she would be the centrepiece of the whole election strategy. She made terrible mistakes, but what broke May's momentum and discredited the Tories' programme was the fact that the Labour leadership was energetically challenging the logic of neoliberalism and proposing a different way of doing things. This is why those who argue that Labour would have done well in the election whoever was leading it, or that it should dial back its radicalism, are profoundly wrong. Labour's sudden surge was precisely a product of the fact that it was only in the election period that people got to know Corbyn and what he stood for and started to realise that there was, at last, a radical alternative on offer in the mainstream.

The struggle between the right embedded in Labour's apparatus and the parliamentary party, and the growing, radicalised membership, is the contemporary expression of a long-term contradiction at Labour's heart. The party has always been shaped by the aspirations and the anger of working people on the one hand, and on the other by the fact that it is focused on gaining office, working with and within the institutions of the British state. It is important to recognise though, that the metrics of this contradiction change over time. In the boom years the Labour party had some leeway to make reforms, especially when under pressure from below. In these circumstances, some kind of left/right accommodation was possible, if not always comfortable. As British capitalism has weakened, the room for compromise and manoeuvre has narrowed. The insurgent nature of Corbyn's rise expresses the fact that the rejection of Labour's recent past is taking place in circumstances in which a change of course would involve a monumental challenge to the status quo. Demands for nationalisation of utilities, an improved welfare state, more progressive taxation and so forth, which could be reluctantly conceded in boom times, imply a more profound confrontation with the structures of class power at a time of sclerotic growth and a worldwide race to the bottom in search of shrinking profits. One outcome of this is that Corbyn is still up against a Labour right that has made its peace with neoliberalism and is no mood to change the course of British society. This struggle, shaped as it is by Labour's position in society and its historical role, cannot be resolved in our favour solely at the level of parliamentary politics.

An exclusive focus on electoral change carries risks in general. The project of trying to win power through the ballot box by appealing to a more or less passive electorate creates the temptation to bend to public opinion – or a caricatured version of it – rather than actively campaigning to try and shape it. This pressure, combined with relentless attacks by Labour's right, has already taken its toll. It has encouraged some on the soft left to try and sound the retreat on 'controversial' policies like scrapping Trident, opposing foreign wars and defending freedom of movement. These are mistakes that can come back to haunt the left. Any effective movement for change needs to work relentlessly to raise people's understanding of the sources of oppression and, in particular the links between racism, nationalism and militarism. If it doesn't it will always be vulnerable to calls to order. The anti-war arguments that have been won by the movements, and were courageously reiterated by Jeremy Corbyn during the June 2017 election, were crucial to blocking Theresa May's attempts to generate a wave of reaction after the terrorist attacks in Manchester and London Bridge.

Most fundamentally though, events of the last two years have raised the question of where power in society really lies and what constitutes a counter-power. The Labour right's campaign of subversion has been aided and abetted by much of the media and other parts of the establishment. Sections of the media have become organising centres for anti-Corbyn manoeuvres. Anti-Corbyn politicians and senior establishment figures have regularly been given air time to explain why

Corbyn can't be trusted with power. One unnamed General told an *Observer* journalist that there would be a mutiny in the armed forces if Corbyn was elected, unless he learnt to love NATO and the nuclear bomb.[3] The efforts at obstruction and sabotage that we have seen at the time of writing will be mild compared to the kind of campaign that will be unleashed if Corbyn gets anywhere near office with a radical programme intact.

The array of forces lined up to defend the status quo, the depths of the crisis faced by the capitalist class and the sheer scale of the resulting assault on working people underline the fact that no electoral project could possibly deal with the task of changing the direction of society on its own. New left electoral parties have emerged recently in many countries in Europe, notably in Portugal, France, Germany, Spain and Greece. They have played an important role in popularizing progressive policy, channeling discontent leftwards and pushing back the right. The intervention by Jean Luc Melenchon's France Insoumise in the recent French presidential elections was looked decisive in slowing the advance of the fascist Front National for instance. In Spain Podemos has helped to give popular expression to the values and concerns of a wide range of social movements. But in some quarters strong claims are being made that these kind of parties are sufficient vehicles for popular control of society. Among many others socialist writers Leo Panitch and Sam Gindin put them at the centre of 'a democratic socialist strategy for entering the state through elections to the end of transforming the state'.[4] But a strategy that is based primarily on trying to implement socialism through parliament – even with mass support – faces a tangle of problems which Panitch and Ginden themselves describe well:

The contradiction for any radical government that would be engaged in this process will include responsibilities for managing a capitalist economy that is likely in crisis while simultaneously trying to satisfy popular expectations for promised relief, and yet also embarking on the longer-term commitment to transform the state.[5]

Mass politics

Embedded as it is in the bourgeois state, parliament institutionalises the debilitating separation between economics and politics. The big corporations and banks that control our economy operate almost completely outside of parliamentary control, and the main institutions of the state that represent their interests are equally unaccountable.

The limitations of a strategy for change through the institutions can only be overcome by popular mobilisations that can push change forward and guard against compromise, backtracking or state repression.

The huge enthusiasm for Corbyn shows there is already a gathering rejection of neoliberalism in Britain that is the product of working-class experience and protest. An effective anti-capitalist strategy must start here. The left needs to focus on the construction of the widest possible movements of resistance and work to rebuild working-class confidence and combativity. This does not mean ignoring the importance of parliament. Far from it, any attempt to transform society in democracies will inevitably have a strong parliamentary component. It involves amongst other things building the widest possible movements in support of parliamentary initiatives, but it is essential not to reduce mass politics to what happens in parliament and to ensure that popular movements are not subordinated to any parliamentary project.

This raises organisational issues. Parties prioritizing parliamentary work are not suited to the task of organising the popular forces needed to overcome their own inertia, isolation or incorporation. In the case of Greece, the left reformist Syriza party spectacularly derailed aspirations for change. This experience, in the European country that has faced the most intense crisis, is particularly instructive. It revealed both the capacity of mass movements to change politics *and* the dangers of falling back on the parliamentary process as the main lever to transform society. In 2010, mass anti-austerity protests sparked a series of demonstrations and strikes that discredited the government and sidelined PASOK, the 'traditional' social democratic party. The movement's main political expression, Syriza, was catapulted into government in the elections of 2015. But by the time Syriza took office, the tide of popular protest had receded. Separated from its base and under pressure from national and international elites, the leadership gave in to the austerity demands of the neoliberal institutions of the EU, even though they had been rejected in a popular referendum. For one of the leaders of Syriza's left at the time, Stathis Kouvelakis, one of the main lessons of the experience was that:

the political practice of radical-left parties vitally needs to articulate parliamentary politics with popular mobilizations; when the second is lost, the first becomes weightless, and actually reinforces the ongoing collapse of representative politics.[6]

Socialist strategy rests most securely on the insight that capitalism draws together and organises human forces with the interest and leverage to challenge its power through self-activity. Concentrated at the heart of the corporate machine and in all the strategic institutions of the system, working people can become agents of self-liberation through their collective and active opposition to the system. Defensive movements are often dismissed as being too reactive or partial to help generate an effective broader challenge. In *Inventing the Future*, Srnicek and Williams, for example, provide a useful critique of the idea that 'spontaneous' struggles *automatically* challenge the status quo. This is a welcome corrective to the idea that capitalism will automatically generate revolutionary 'events' that will somehow transform society of their own accord. All struggle, all resistance is organised, and as well as ignoring this obvious point, the romanticisation of spontaneous struggle fatally downplays the importance of strategy and co-ordination. But *Inventing the Future* ends up dismissing reactive struggle altogether, arguing against an 'emphasis on resistance' and that, 'demands to "save our health system" or "stop austerity"...simply reveal a conservative disposition at the heart of a movement'.[7] This is to ignore recurring dynamics in mass resistance. Almost all great social struggles, from the Russian Revolution to the Spanish Civil War, from the Civil Rights movement in the USA to the recent uprisings in Tunisia and Egypt, start out with defensive moves.

From the anti-Nazi league in the late 1970s to the miners' support campaign in the 1980s, from the poll tax protests in the 1990s to the anti-war and the anti-austerity campaigns more recently, mass movements have had a profound impact on British life. Their combination of mass participation and publicity value has radically influenced the ideas circulating in society. The anti-war movement failed to stop the Iraq War, but it has made it much harder for subsequent governments to start new ones. Con Coughlin, defence editor of *The Daily Telegraph*, recently wrote a column complaining about the influence of the Stop the War Coalition:

> Its relentless propaganda campaign – and downright lies – relating to the recent military campaigns in Iraq and Afghanistan has achieved its goal of turning public opinion and parliament against initiating any further military interventions.[8]

He was wrong about the lies but broadly correct about the

influence. Mass movements can also provide a practical answer to the doubts people have about their ability to influence events. Participating in any big protest boosts confidence, winning victories is transformative.

Once the cycle of resistance has begun, the experience of mass struggle can clarify more quickly and comprehensively than anything else the hostile nature of the institutions of capitalist society, and the creative potential stored up in the 'ordinary' population. If the struggle deepens, the need for more fundamental transformation can very quickly become clear.

It is in the midst of this process that socialists have the best chance of proving the value of their ideas and their approach and of developing a really popular programme for change in collaboration with working people – the only type of socialist programme that matters.

The importance of the united front in bringing together the most radical activists with much wider forces was elaborated at length at the third and fourth congresses of the Communist International in the early 1920s, in particular in the contributions of Leon Trotsky.[9] Italian Marxist Antonio Gramsci took up the idea in his *Prison Notebooks*, an attempt to grapple with the problems of transformation in 'advanced' Western capitalism. For Gramsci such systematic united action was necessary to construct an alliance led by working people that had the weight to undermine ruling-class hegemony and challenge for power. But he also argued that such collaboration in struggle was essential for the renewal of socialist ideas and theory. Only people actively and passionately engaged in trying to change the world can identify the elements in the situation which can take the struggle forward. This is the practical meaning of the central idea that socialist theory is the crystallization of the experience of working people. 'It is not,' Gramsci argued, 'a question of introducing from scratch a scientific form of thought into everyone's individual life, but of renovating and making "critical" an already existing activity'.[10]

More than that movements from below can, in fact, be critical to resolving the problem of popular representation. We have seen that Corbyn's rise is itself a product of the movements, just as Jeremy Corbyn wouldn't be where he was without his connection with mass campaigns, the left in Labour will only make further headway if it is backed up by popular protest. Protests will be needed to help push forward the radicalisation in society, to defend the left against the right in Labour, and to deal with state hostility. Even maintaining radical positions on immigration, capping high pay, renationalisation, and so forth, will depend more than anything on the movement's ability to keep mobilising. And, given the scale of opposition it would face, a radical left government would only have a chance of making any progress if it was backed by systematically organised popular mobilisations.

Class opposition will ultimately have to find forms of democracy that can serve it better than parliament. Historically, at their insurrectionary high points, mass struggles have thrown up new forms of popular democracy embedded in the everyday life of working people that have the potential to overcome the separation of politics and economics. After the Russian Revolution, workers', peasants' and soldiers' councils spread across swathes of Europe, drawing together re-callable delegates from workplaces, communities and the radicalised garrisons in assemblies that became centres of popular power. Similar bodies have emerged in many of the insurgent movements that have followed, from Hungary in 1956, Chile and Portugal in the early 1970s to the first period of the Iranian Revolution in 1979 to Argentinian and Bolivian insurgencies in the last decade. All of these institutions emerged initially out of the immediate needs of defensive, reactive struggles at times of great crisis. But in different ways and to different degrees they allowed ordinary people to begin to run their own affairs – political, social and economic – themselves. A decisive further struggle is needed to confront and disable the institutions of the capitalist state, but variants of such highly democratic, participatory bodies are the indispensable basis for that final reckoning.

Ideas and action

As Marx proposed in the *Communist Manifesto*, there should be no distinction between the interests of socialists and those of the wider movement.[11] But there *are* always discussions and debates about what strategy is most effective to take the movement forward. The limitations of a purely reformist strategy for change are not always obvious. Even within active movements there is a strong pressure to prioritise electioneering or see protest as little more than an add-on to the real political business taking place in parliament. To help build the strongest possible movements, those convinced of the need for a fundamental change from below need to organise together politically at the same time as strengthening resistance. The experience of life under capitalism radicalises, but within certain limits. Even at high points of struggle, elements of division and passivity remain. People's experience remains partial and particular. Various forms of oppression are used to divide people and try and set them against each other. The sense of powerlessness that comes from having so little control over daily life lingers in even the most intense social crisis and this sense is reinforced by endless propaganda. Opposition can be deflected and co-opted by establishment institutions and by labour movement bodies that have been partially incorporated.

For all these reasons, organisation of the most radical and revolutionary is needed to integrate the partial insights thrown up in day to day struggles into a rounded picture of the way the system operates, to counter the idea that change can be delivered simply by electing better people to parliament and to develop and continually modify a strategy of change. Socialist activists are needed in every workplace and community with the confidence to counter elite propaganda and encourage the boldest possible working-class organisation and resistance. This intellectual and organisational effort involves not just generalising contemporary experience but bringing to bear the best of the revolutionary tradition on the present. It would be foolish to grapple with the task of making change happen without absorbing the lessons of resistance in the past. Socialist theory is nothing but this; the condensed experience of the long tradition of anti-capitalist struggle. Without such an organised, conscious revolutionary pole within the mass movements, the steps from resistance to transformation will never be taken. But once organised together, socialists need to look outwards again and connect with people way beyond their ranks. This is clearly not a moment to be downhearted, but nor is it a moment for cheering from the sidelines. A time of system failure and class-based discontent is a time to take the initiative.

Endnotes

Introduction: Surprise, Surprise

1. Quoted in Kouvelakis, S. (2003), *Philosophy and Revolution*, p.48
2. Davies, W. (2014), *The Limits of Neoliberalism: Authority, Sovereignty and the Logic of Competition*, p.190.
3. Münchau, W., 'The Elites' Marie Antoinette Moment', *Financial Times*, 27 November 2016.
4. Some of these essays are collected in Hall, J. and Jacques, M. (eds.) (1989), *New Times, the Changing Face of Politics in the 1990s*.
5. Nineham, C. (1995), 'Is the media all powerful?', *International Socialism*, 67, p.117.
6. Jameson, F. (2005), *Archaeologies of the Future: The Desire called Utopia and other Science Fictions*.
7. Quotes from Marx, K., 'A contribution to the Critique of Hegel's Philosophy of Right and Theses on Feuerbach', *Marx, Early Writings*, (1975) pp.256, 422.

1. We Never Bought the Dream

1. Lenin, V.I. (1905), 'Reorganisation of the party', *Selected Works* Vol 3 (1942) p.459.
2. Fukuyama, F., 'The End of History?' *National Interest* Summer 1989, p.15.
3. Frank, T. (2000) *One Market Under God*, p.xiii.
4. Interview with *Women's Own* 1987, quoted in 'Margaret Thatcher: a life in quotes', *The Guardian*, 8 April 2013.
5. Mort, F. (1988), 'The Politics of Consumption' in Hall, S., and Jacques, M. (eds.), *New Times: The Changing Face of Politics in the 1990s*, p.170.
6. Hall, S. (1988), 'The Meaning of New Times' in Chen, K-H. and Morley, D. (eds.) *Stuart Hall: Critical Dialogues in*

Cultural Studies, p.227.

7. Peck, J. (2010) *Constructions of Neoliberal Reason*, p.xi.

8. See in particular Peck, J. (2010) above, and Mirowski, P. (2013), *Never Let a Serious Crisis Go to Waste: How Neoliberalism Survived the Financial Meltdown*.

9. Gamble, A. (1981), *Britain in Decline*, p.7.

10. Gamble, A. (1981), as above, pp.19–20.

11. Riddell, P. (1983), *The Thatcher Government*, p.59.

12. Cliff, T. (1996), *The Labour Party: A Marxist History*, p.325.

13. Quoted in Cliff, T. (1996), as above, p.322.

14. Field, F., 'How the Poor Fared' in Coates, K. (eds.) (1979), *What Went Wrong?* p.105.

15. Cliff, T. (1996), as above, p.330.

16. Foot, P. (2005), *The Vote: How it Was Won and How it Was Undermined*, p.396.

17. Ipsos MORI *Margaret Thatcher: Public Opinion Trends*, 8 April 2013, available at: https://www.ipsos-mori.com/researchpublications/researcharchive/3158/Margaret-Thatcher-19252013.aspx

18. Gallup Political Poll Index number 256 December 1981, p.2, quoted in Cliff, T. (1996), p.354.

19. Hobsbawn, E., (1989), *Politics for a Rational Left*, p.164.

20. Bale, T. (2010), *The Conservative Party from Thatcher to Cameron*, p.23.

21. Milne, S. (2004), *The Enemy Within: The Secret War against the Miners*.

22. Moore, C. (2005), *Margaret Thatcher: The Authorized Biography, Volume Two: Everything She Wants*, p.2.

23. *Daily Mirror*, 19 October 1986, quoted in Cliff, T. (1996), p.359.

24. *Financial Times*, 2 October 1987, quoted in Cliff, T. (1996) p.359.

25. Cliff, T. (1996), as above, p.375

26. Curtice, J., 'Interim Report: Party Politics' in *The British*

Social Attitudes Survey, (1987), p.174.

27. Heath A., Jowell, R. and Curtice, J. (1994), *Labour's Last Chance? The 1992 Election and Beyond*, p.285.

28. Heath A., Jowell, R. and Curtice, J. (1994), as above, p.196.

29. *The British Social Attitudes Survey* quoted in Cousins, A., 'The Crisis of the British Regime: Democracy, Protest and the Unions', 27 November 2011, available at http://www.counterfire.org/theory/37-theory/14906-the-crisis-of-the-british-regime-democracy-protest-and-the-unions#institutions

30. Heffernan, R. and Marqusee, M. (1992) *Defeat from the Jaws of Victory: Inside Kinnock's Labour Party*, p.265–77.

31. Conservative Home, 'Margaret Thatcher's Greatest Achievement: New Labour', 11 April 2008, available at: http://conservativehome.blogs.com/centreright/2008/04/making-history.html

2. The Second Death of Liberal England

1. BBC News, 'Tony Blair: 'My job was to build on some Thatcher policies', 8 April 2013. Available at: http://www.bbc.co.uk/news/uk-politics-22073434

2. See for example Muller, J., 'The Populist Moment' in *London Review of Books*, 1 December 2016, pp.10–11.

3. Liddle, R. and Mandelson, P. (1996), *The Blair Revolution, Can New Labour Deliver?*

4. Hay, C. (1999), *The Political Economy of New Labour*

5. Dorling, D. (2015), *Inequality and the 1%*, p.19.

6. Foot, P. (2005), as above, p.424.

7. Foot, P. (2005), as above, p.417.

8. Dorling, D. (2011), *Injustice: Why Social Inequality Persists*, p.191.

9. Reed, H. (2011), *Fairness and Prosperity*, p.5, available at: https://www.tuc.org.uk/sites/default/files/tucfiles/fairnessandprosperity.pdf

10. Dorling, D. (2015), as above, pp.91,191.
11. Mustafa, J., *Daily Telegraph*, 29 August 2016, available at: http://www.telegraph.co.uk/news/2016/08/29/more-than-700-civil-servants-officials-and-quangocrats-earned-mo
12. Dorling, D. (2011), as above, p.189.
13. Dorling, D. (2011), as above, p.189.
14. Harvey, D. (2005), *A Brief History of Neoliberalism*, p.59.
15. Dorling, D. (2015), as above, pp.114,189.
16. Harvey, D. (2005), as above, p.160.
17. Davies, W., 'The home office rules', *London Review of Books*, 3 November 2016, p.6.
18. Counterfire.org, quoted in Cousins, A., 'The Crisis of the British Regime', 27 November 2011, available at: http://www.counterfire.org/theory/37-theory/14906-the-crisis-of-the-british-regime-democracy-protest-and-the-unions
19. Bale, T. and Webb, P., 'Members Only: Views of the Conservative Party's Rank and File', Political Studies Association, available at: https://www.psa.ac.uk/insight-plus/members-only-views-conservative-party's-rank-and-file
20. Gieve, J.,'The Puzzle of UK Business Investment', The Bank of England website, 26 September 2006, available at: http://www.bankofengland.co.uk/archive/Documents/historicpubs/speeches/2006/speech282.pdf
21. Office for National Statistics, 'Gross Capital Formation and Business Investment', Economics Online, available here: http://www.economicsonline.co.uk/Managing_the_economy/Investment.html
22. Harvey, D. (2005), as above, pp.155,161.
23. Norfield, T. (2016), *The City, London and the Power of Global Finance*, p.108.
24. McKibbin, R., 'Money and the Love of Money', *London Review of Books*, 2 August 2012, p.6.
25. Dorling, D. (2015), as above, p.90.

26. Norfield, T. (2016), as above, p.134.
27. *Changing Banking for Good*, Parliamentary Commission on Banking Standards Report, 2013-2014, p.12.
28. 'UKIP Supporters say tackling rich/poor gap is higher priority than taxes and benefits', High Pay Centre, 22 April 2014, available here: http://highpaycentre.org/blog/ukip-supporters-say-tackling-rich-poor-gap-is-higher-priority-than-taxes-an
29. Streeck, W., (2014), How Will Capitalism End? In *New Left Review* 87, May–June 2014. Available at: https://newleftreview.org/II/87/wolfgang-streeck-how-will-capitalism-end
30. Norfield, T. (2016), as above, p.151.
31. Streeck, W. (2014), as above.
32. See for instance, 'Annual Reports and Accounts 2015–2016', Ministry of Defence, p.8, available at: https://www.gov.uk/government/uploads/system/uploads/attachment_data/file/558559/MoD_AR16.pdf
33. Steele, J., 'Trouble at the FCO', *London Review of Books*, 28 July 2016, p.10.
34. Muttit, G. (2012), *Fuel on the Fire: Oil and Politics in Occupied Iraq*
35. 'UK Attacked Iraq for Oil – Poll', War on Want, 10 March 2008, available here: http://www.waronwant.org/media/uk-attacked-iraq-oil-poll
36. Curtis, M., 'Britain's Seven Covert Wars', Huffington Post, 18 October 2016, available here: http://www.huffingtonpost.co.uk/mark-curtis/britains-seven-covert-war_b_12332368.html
37. Suskind, R., 'Faith, Certainty and the Presidency of George W. Bush.' *The New York Times Magazine*, 17 October 2004, available here: http://www.nytimes.com/2004/10/17/magazine/faith-certainty-and-the-presidency-of-george-w-bush.html

38. Oborne, P. (2007) *The Triumph of the Political Class* p. xviii.

39. 'Blair Warns of Duty to Integrate' Politics.co.uk, 8 December 2006, available here: http://www.politics.co.uk/news/2006/12/8/blair-warns-of-duty-to-integrate

40. Streeck, W. (2014), as above.

3. The Sound of Cracking

1. Quoted in Jones, O. (2015), *The Establishment: And how they get away with it*, p. 65.

2. 'The Problem of Trust', YouGov UK, 13 November 2012, available at: https://yougov.co.uk/news/2012/11/13/problem-trust/

3. Eurobarometer Survey, quoted in Cousins, A., 'The Crisis of the British Regime', Counterfire.org, 27 November 2011, available at: http://www.counterfire.org/theory/37-theory/14906-the-crisis-of-the-british-regime-democracy-protest-and-the-unions

4. 'General Election Turnout 1945–2015', Political Info, available at: http://www.ukpolitical.info/Turnout45.htm

5. Lloyd, J., 'After the Fact', *Financial Times, Life and arts*, 27 May 2017, p.8.

6. Kay, J., 'How our politicians fell out of love with the market' *Financial Times*, 20 May 2017, p.12.

7. 'Trust, Politics and Institutions', *British Social Attitudes Survey 2013*, available at: http://www.bsa.natcen.ac.uk/latest-report/british-social-attitudes-30/key-findings/trust-politics-and-institutions.aspx

8. See graph 18 in, Cousins, A., 'The Crisis of the British Regime', Counterfire.org, 27 November 2011, available at: http://www.counterfire.org/theory/37-theory/14906-the-crisis-of-the-british-regime-democracy-protest-and-the-unions

9. Quoted in Cousins, A., 'The Crisis of the British Regime', as above.

10. Quote and figures from, 'How Far is Public Opinion from the Political Centre Ground?' *Journalism From Mars*, 26 January, 2015. Available at: https://journalismfrommars. co.uk/2015/01/26/how-far-is-public-opinion-from-the-political-centre-ground/

11. Quoted in Jones, O. (2015), as above, p.65.

12. 'Labour's Beckett Report busts myths about why the party lost the 2015 general election', *The Independent*, 19 January 2016, available at: http://www.independent.co.uk/news/uk/politics/commonly-believed-reasons-why-labour-lost-the-election-arent-significant-says-partys-beckett-report-a6821476.html

13. Both surveys quoted in Cousins, A., 'The Crisis of the British Regime', as above

14. 'Socialism more popular with British people than capitalism, survey finds', *The Independent*, 23 February 2016, available at: http://www.independent.co.uk/news/uk/politics/socialism-is-more-popular-with-the-british-public-than-capitalism-survey-finds-a6892371.html

15. Bale, T., Webb, P. and Peletti, M., 'Ideology is in the Eye of the Beholder: How British party supporters see themselves, their parties, and their rivals', LSE website, 8 January 2016, available at: http://blogs.lse.ac.uk/politicsandpolicy/ideology-is-in-the-eye-of-the-beholder/

16. 'Majority support for rail nationalisation – but also policies from the 'radical' right', YouGov UK, 6 August 2015.,available at: https://yougov.co.uk/news/2015/08/06/support-radical-left-and-right/

17. Quoted in 'How Far is Public Opinion form the Political Centre ground?' *Journalism From Mars*, 26 January, 2015, available at: https://journalismfrommars.co.uk/2015/01/26/how-far-is-public-opinion-from-the-political-centre-ground/

18. Gribble, R. and Wessley S. (2014), 'British Public Opinion after a Decade of War: Attitudes to Iraq and Afghanistan',

Politics 2014. Available at: https://www.kcl.ac.uk/kcmhr/ publications/assetfiles/2014/Gribble2014b.pdf

19. Wintour, P., 'Multicultural Britain rejecting foreign conflict, MoD admits', *The Guardian*, 23 January 2014, available at: https://www.theguardian.com/uk-news/2014/jan/22/ multicultural-britain-foreign-conflict-mod

20. Walgrave, S. and Rucht, D. (2010), *The World Says No to War: Demonstrations Against the War on Iraq*, p.24.

21. 'How Scotland voted, and why', Lord Ashcroft Polls, 19 September, 2014, available at: http://lordashcroftpolls. com/2014/09/scotland-voted/

22. Lord Ashcroft Polls, 19 September 2014, as above.

23. 'The confused commentariat wants to pin all of Corbyn's success on the young, which isn't just wrong – it's dangerous', *The Independent*, 13 June 2017, available at http://www.independent.co.uk/voices/jeremy-corbyn-labour-success-youth-young-vote-msm-commentariat-wrong-dangerous-a7787301.html

24. Holder, J., Kommenda, N., Barr, C. and Clarke, S. 'How did Theresa May's gamble fail?', The Guardian, 9 June, 2017, available at https://www.theguardian.com/politics/ ng-interactive/2017/jun/09/theresa-may-election-gamble-fail-conservatives-majority-polls

25. 'How the War on Terror coverage affected the UK vote'. *The Listening Post*, Al Jazeera, broadcast 12 June 2017, available at: http://www.aljazeera.com/programmes/ listeningpost/2017/06/war-terror-coverage-affected-uk-vote-170610102440856.html

26. Quoted in Merrick, R. 'Jeremy Corbyn blames terrorist attacks such as Manchester bombing on UK foreign policy'. *The Independent*, 25 May 2017, available at: *http://www. independent.co.uk/news/uk/politics/jeremy-corbyn-manchester-attack-terrorism-uk-foreign-policy-wars-speech-a7756266.html*

27. Freedland, J.,'The Corbyn tribe cares about identity, not

power', *The Guardian*, 24 July 2015, available at: https://www.theguardian.com/commentisfree/2015/jul/24/corbyn-tribe-identity-politics-labour

28. MaCaskill, A., 'Revealed: How Jeremy Corbyn has reshaped the Labour Party', *The Guardian*, 13 January 2016, available at: https://www.theguardian.com/politics/2016/jan/13/revealed-how-jeremy-corbyn-has-reshaped-the-labour-party

And, Stone, J., 'Jeremy Corbyn's supporters are more working class than other candidates', research finds', *The Independent*, 28 August 2015, available at: http://www.independent.co.uk/news/uk/politics/jeremy-corbyns-supporters-are-more-working-class-than-other-candidates-research-finds-10476433.html

29. Gilbert, J., 'Postmodernity and the crisis of democracy', Open Democracy, 28 May 2009, available at: https://www.opendemocracy.net/article/opendemocracy-theme/postmodernity-and-the-crisis-of-democracy

30. Stone, J., 'Tony Blair says he wouldn't want a left-wing Labour party to win an election' *The Independent*, 22 July 2015, available at: http://www.independent.co.uk/news/uk/politics/tony-blair-says-he-wouldn-t-want-a-left-wing-labour-party-to-win-an-election-10406928.html

31. '48:52 – Healing a Divided Britain', Legatum Institute, 1 October 2016, p.2, available at: https://lif.blob.core.windows.net/lif/docs/default-source/publications/48-52-healing-a-divided-nation-october-2016-pdf.pdf?sfvrsn=2

32. Becker, S.O., Fetzer, T. and Novy. D. (2016), Who Voted for Brexit?', pp.38–9. Available at: http://www2.warwick.ac.uk/fac/soc/economics/research/centres/cage/manage/news/305-2016_becker_fetzer_novy.pdf

33. 'How the United Kingdom voted on Thursday...and why', Lord Ashcroft Polls, 24 June 2016, available at: http://lordashcroftpolls.com/2016/06/how-the-united-kingdom-voted-and-why/

34. '48:52 – Healing a Divided Britain', Legatum Institute, as above, p.12.

35. 'Making a success of Brexit', CBI, December 2016, available at: http://www.cbi.org.uk/news/uk-needs-a-whole-economy-approach-to-make-a-success-of-brexit/

36. 'How the United Kingdom voted on Thursday...and why', Lord Ashcroft Polls as above.

37. Gramsci, A. (1971), *Selections from the Prison Notebooks*, p.57.

4. The Poverty of Propaganda

1. Eagleton, T. (1991), *Ideology: an Introduction*, p.xiv.

2. Kishi, H., 'Media Concentration: A Crisis of Democracy', 7 August, 2014. Media Reform Coalition. Available at: http://www.mediareform.org.uk/media-ownership/media-concentration-crisis-democracy

3. 'News consumption in the UK: Research report', 15 December 2015, *Ofcom*. Available at: https://www.ofcom.org.uk/__data/assets/pdf_file/0020/77222/News-2015-report.pdf

4. Myerscough, P., 'Corbyn in the Media', *London Review of Books*, 2 October 2015, p.9.

5. BBC *Newsnight*, 9 June 2015, available at: http://www.leftfutures.org/dev05082015/2015/06/jeremy-corbyn-makes-his-pitch-for-the-labour-leadership-on-newsnight/

6. See, Cammaerts, B., Brooks, D., Magalhães, J. and Jimenez-Martínez, C., 'Journalistic Representations of Jeremy Corbyn in the British Press: From Watchdog to Attackdog', 1 July 2016. *London School of Economics and Political Science.* Available at: http://www.lse.ac.uk/media@lse/research/pdf/JeremyCorbyn/Cobyn-Report.pdf
And 'What the BBC has to say about the papers' 5 June, 2017. *Media Reform Coalition.* Available at: http://www.mediareform.org.uk/blog/bbc-say-papers

7. Mortimer, C. 'Stephen Doughty: Labour MP's on-air

resignation 'prearranged by the BBC' *The Independent,* 8 January 2016. Available at: http://www.independent. co.uk/news/uk/politics/stephen-doughty-labour-mps-jeremy-corbyn-on-air-resignation-prearranged-by-the-bbc-a6801846.html

8. 'Why we believe this country needs a strong Conservative team as the next government'. *London Evening Standard,* 7 June 2017, p.16.

9. Stone, J. 'Jeremy Corbyn media coverage deliberately biased against him, British public believes'. *The Independent,* 4 September 2016. Available at: http://www.independent. co.uk/news/uk/politics/jeremy-corbyn-poll-labour-leadership-media-bias-believe-against-him-supporters-mi5-portland-a7225031.html

10. Chomsky, N. (1989), *Necessary Illusions,* p.10.

11. Herman, E., 'The Propaganda Model Revisited', *Monthly Review,* 11 July 1996, p.8.

12. Herman, E., as above, p.6.

13. Anderson, P. (1976), *Considerations of Western Marxism,* p.75.

14. Horkheimer, M. and Adorno, T.W. (1973), *The Dialectic of the Enlightenment,* and Marcuse, H. (1964), *One-Dimensional Man: Studies in the Ideology of Advanced Industrial Society*

15. Interview with Foucault quoted in Wollin, R. (2010), *The Wind from the East: French Intellectuals, the Cultural Revolution and the Legacy of the 1960s,* p.326.

16. Foucault, M. (1990), A *History of Sexuality Volume 1,* p.96 .

17. Ahmad, A. (1992), *In Theory: Classes, Nations, Literatures,* p.185.

18. Norris, C. (1992), *Uncritical Theory: Postmodernism, Intellectuals and the Gulf War* p.96.

19. Baudrillard, J. (1995), *The Gulf War Did Not Take Place.*

20. Fisher, M. (2009), *Capitalist Realism,* p.9.

21. Quoted in Davies, N. (2009), *Flat Earth News,* p.329.

22. Marx, K. (1970), *The German Ideology,* p.64.

23. Marx, K. (1981), *Capital, Vol 3*, p.311.
24. Lukács, G. (1971) *History and Class Consciousness*, p.90.
25. Lukács, G. (1971), as above, p.100.
26. Jakubowski, F. (1976), *Ideology and Superstructure in Historical Materialism*, p.115.
27. Lukács, G. (1971), as above, p.92.. Lukács, G. (1971), as above, pp.74–5.
28. Lukács, G. (1971), as above, pp.74–5.
29. Luxemburg, R. (1986), *The Mass Strike*, p.38.
30. Marx, K. (1970), as above, p.95.

5. Where Are the Workers?

1. Quoted in Todd, S. (2014), *The People: The Rise and Fall of the Working Class*, p.339.
2. Quotes from Todd, S. (2014), as above, pp.339–40.
3. Todd, S. (2014), as above, pp.340–41.
4. Standing, G. (2011), *The Precariat: The New Dangerous Class*, p.vii.
5. 'The Great British Calculator: What Class are you?' BBC News, 3 April 2013. Available at: http://www.bbc.co.uk/news/magazine-22000973
6. Bourdieu, P. (1986), *The Forms of Capital*.
7. For a discussion of this see for example, Wood, E. M. (1986), *The Retreat from Class: A New 'True' Socialism*.
8. Mason, P. (2015), *PostCapitalism: A Guide to our Future*, p.179.
9. Srnicek, N. and Williams, A. (2015), *Inventing the Future: Postcapitalism and a World Without Work*, Chapter 5.
10. Palmer, B.D. 'Reconsiderations of class: Precariousness as proletarianization', *Socialist Register* 2014, p.57, available at: http://www.leftforum.org/sites/default/files/panel_documents/PalmerSR2014.pdf
11. 'Trade Union Membership 2015', Department for Business, Innovation and Skills, p.12, available at: https://www.gov.

uk/government/uploads/system/uploads/attachment_data/ file/525938/Trade_Union_Membership_2015_-_Statistical_ Bulletin.pdf

12. Rhodes, C., 'Manufacturing Statistics and Policy', House of Commons Briefing Paper, 6, August 2015, p.8.

13. 'Employment Rate', Office for National Statistics, 14 December 2016, available at: https://www.ons.gov. uk/employmentandlabourmarket/peopleinwork/ employmentandemployeetypes/timeseries/lf24/lms

14. German, L. (1996), A Question of Class, p.27.

15. Todd, S. (2014), as above, p.14.

16. Dunn, B. (2011), 'The new economy and labour's decline: questioning their association', in Serrano, M., Xhafa, E. and Fichter, M. (eds.), Trade unions and the global crisis: Labours visions, strategies and responses, p.67.

17 Marx, K. (1976), Capital Vol 1, p.797.

18. Jenkins, S.P. (2000), 'Dynamics of Household Incomes' in Berthoud, R et al (eds) Seven Years in the Lives of British Families: Evidence on the Dynamics of Social Change p.127.

19. 'Measuring Economic Precarity among UK Youth during the Depression', ESRC Centre for Population Change, November 2014, available at: http://www.cpc.ac.uk/ publications/cpc_briefing_papers/pdf/BP22_Measuring_ economic_precarity.pdf

20. 'State of the Nation: Where is Bittersweet Britain Heading?' British Future 2013, p.3, available at: http://www. britishfuture.org/wp-content/uploads/2013/01/State-of-the-Nation-2013.pdf

21. Todd, S. (2014), as above, p.357.

22. German, L. (1996), as above, p.27.

23. 'How Have Employees Fared?' Employment Relations Research Series, no 56, Recent UK Trends, 2006, p7, available at: www.dti.gov.uk/publications

24 Godard, J. (2011), 'What has happened to strikes?', British

Journal of Industrial Relations, June 2011, p. 297.

25 See graph 22, Cousins, A., 'The Crisis of the British Regime: Democracy, Protest and the Unions', 27 November 2011, available at http://www.counterfire.org/theory/37-theory/14906-the-crisis-of-the-british-regime-democracy-protest-and-the-unions#institutions

26. Bailey, D.J., 'Hard Evidence: This is the Age of Dissent and there is much more to come', The Conversation, 11 January 2016, available at: https://theconversation.com/hard-evidence-this-is-the-age-of-dissent-and-theres-much-more-to-come-52871

27. Norris, P. (2003), *Young People & Political Activism: From the Politics of Loyalties to the Politics of Choice?*

28. Norris, P. (2003), *Democratic Phoenix,* p.193.

29. Nunn, A. (2016), *The Candidate: Jeremy Corbyn's Improbable Path to Power*, p.145.

30. 'Majority Support Doctors Ahead of First Full Walkout', Ipsos MORI, 25 April 2016. Available at: https://www.ipsos-mori.com/researchpublications/researcharchive/3727/Majority-support-junior-doctors-ahead-of-first-full-walkout.aspx

6. Socialists and System Failure

1. Le Guin, U. K., *The Guardian*, 20 November 2014, 'Ursula K Le Guin's speech at National Book Awards: '"Books aren't just commodities."'', available at: https://www.theguardian.com/books/2014/nov/20/ursula-k-le-guin-national-book-awards-speech

2. Streeck, W. (2014), 'How Will Capitalism End?', *New Left Review* 87, May–June 2014, available at: https://newleftreview.org/II/87/wolfgang-streeck-how-will-capitalism-end

3. '"British Army 'could stage mutiny under Corbyn", says senior serving general', *The Independent*, 20 September

2015, available at: http://www.independent.co.uk/news/uk/
politics/british-army-could-stage-mutiny-under-corbyn-
says-senior-serving-general-10509742.html

4. Panitch, L. and Albo, G. (2016) *Rethinking Revolution,*
    Socialist Register 2017, p.54.

5. Panitch, L. and Albo, G. (2016) As above, p.54.

6. Kouvelakis, S. (2016) 'Syriza's Rise and Fall', *New Left
    Review,* 97, available at: https://newleftreview.org/II/97/
    stathis-kouvelakis-syriza-s-rise-and-fall

7. Srnicek, N. and Williams, A. (2015), *Inventing the Future:
    Postcapitalism and a World Without Work,* Chapter 2.

8. Coughlin, C., 'The Stop the War Coalition is Fighting
    on Behalf of Britain's Enemies', *The Daily Telegraph,* 13
    October 2016, available at: http://www.telegraph.co.uk/
    news/2016/10/13/the-stop-the-war-coalition-is-fighting-on-
    behalf-of-britains-ene/

9. See for example, Trotsky, L. (1924) 'On the United Front'
    in Trotsky, L. (1974) *The First Five Years of the Communist
    International,* p.91.

10. Gramsci, A. (1971), *Selections from the Prison Notebooks,*
    p.331.

11. Marx K. and Engels, F. (1848), 'The Communist Manifesto'
    in Marx K. (1973), *The Revolutions of 1848.*

CULTURE, SOCIETY & POLITICS

Contemporary culture has eliminated the concept and public figure of the intellectual. A cretinous anti-intellectualism presides, cheer-led by hacks in the pay of multinational corporations who reassure their bored readers that there is no need to rouse themselves from their stupor. Zer0 Books knows that another kind of discourse - intellectual without being academic, popular without being populist - is not only possible: it is already flourishing. Zer0 is convinced that in the unthinking, blandly consensual culture in which we live, critical and engaged theoretical reflection is more important than ever before. If you have enjoyed this book, why not tell other readers by posting a review on your preferred book site.

Recent bestsellers from Zero Books are

In the Dust of This Planet
Horror of Philosophy vol. 1
Eugene Thacker
In the first of a series of three books on the Horror of Philosophy, *In the Dust of This Planet* offers the genre of horror as a way of thinking about the unthinkable.
Paperback: 978-1-84694-676-9 ebook: 978-1-78099-010-1

Capitalist Realism
Is there no alternative?

Mark Fisher

An analysis of the ways in which capitalism has presented itself as the only realistic political-economic system.

Paperback: 978-1-84694-317-1 ebook: 978-1-78099-734-6

Rebel Rebel
Chris O'Leary

David Bowie: every single song. Everything you want to know, everything you didn't know.

Paperback: 978-1-78099-244-0 ebook: 978-1-78099-713-1

Cartographies of the Absolute
Alberto Toscano, Jeff Kinkle

An aesthetics of the economy for the twenty-first century.

Paperback: 978-1-78099-275-4 ebook: 978-1-78279-973-3

Malign Velocities
Accelerationism and Capitalism

Benjamin Noys

Long listed for the Bread and Roses Prize 2015, *Malign Velocities* argues against the need for speed, tracking acceleration as the symptom of the on-going crises of capitalism.

Paperback: 978-1-78279-300-7 ebook: 978-1-78279-299-4

Meat Market
Female flesh under Capitalism

Laurie Penny

A feminist dissection of women's bodies as the fleshy fulcrum of capitalist cannibalism, whereby women are both consumers and consumed.

Paperback: 978-1-84694-521-2 ebook: 978-1-84694-782-7

Poor but Sexy
Culture Clashes in Europe East and West
Agata Pyzik
How the East stayed East and the West stayed West.
Paperback: 978-1-78099-394-2 ebook: 978-1-78099-395-9

Romeo and Juliet in Palestine
Teaching Under Occupation
Tom Sperlinger
Life in the West Bank, the nature of pedagogy and the role of a
university under occupation.
Paperback: 978-1-78279-637-4 ebook: 978-1-78279-636-7

Sweetening the Pill
or How we Got Hooked on Hormonal Birth Control
Holly Grigg-Spall
Has contraception liberated or oppressed women? *Sweetening the
Pill* breaks the silence on the dark side of hormonal contraception.
Paperback: 978-1-78099-607-3 ebook: 978-1-78099-608-0

Why Are We The Good Guys?
Reclaiming your Mind from the Delusions of Propaganda
David Cromwell
A provocative challenge to the standard ideology that Western
power is a benevolent force in the world.
Paperback: 978-1-78099-365-2 ebook: 978-1-78099-366-9

Readers of ebooks can buy or view any of these bestsellers by
clicking on the live link in the title. Most titles are published in
paperback and as an ebook. Paperbacks are available in traditional
bookshops. Both print and ebook formats are available online.

Find more titles and sign up to our readers' newsletter at
http://www.johnhuntpublishing.com/culture-and-politics
Follow us on Facebook at https://www.facebook.com/ZeroBooks
and Twitter at https://twitter.com/Zer0Books